1st EDITION

Perspectives on Modern World History

The John F. Kennedy Assassination

1st EDITION

Perspectives on Modern World History

The John F. Kennedy Assassination

Sylvia Engdahl

Editor

GREENHAVEN PRESS

A part of Gale, Cengage Learning

GALE
CENGAGE Learning

Detroit • New York • San Francisco • New Haven, Conn • Waterville, Maine • London

GALE
CENGAGE Learning

Christine Nasso, *Publisher*
Elizabeth Des Chenes, *Managing Editor*

For more information, contact:
Greenhaven Press
27500 Drake Rd.
Farmington Hills, MI 48331-3535
Or you can visit our Internet site at gale.cengage.com.

Articles in Greenhaven Press anthologies are often edited for length to meet page requirements. In addition, original titles of these works are changed to clearly present the main thesis and to explicitly indicate the author's opinion. Every effort is made to ensure that Greenhaven Press accurately reflects the original intent of the authors. Every effort has been made to trace the owners of copyrighted material.

Cover image Custom Medical Stock Photo, Inc. Reproduced by permission.

LIBRARY OF CONGRESS CATALOGING-IN-PUBLICATION DATA

The John F. Kennedy assassination / Sylvia Engdahl, book editor.
p. cm. -- (Perspectives on modern world history)
Includes bibliographical references and index.
ISBN 978-0-7377-5006-5 (hardcover)
1. Kennedy, John F. (John Fitzgerald), 1917-1963--Assassination--Juvenile literature. I. Engdahl, Sylvia.
E842.9.J6423 2010
973.922092--dc22 2010017842

Printed in the United States of America
1 2 3 4 5 6 7 14 13 12 11 10

CONTENTS

FOREWORD

"History cannot give us a program for the future, but it can give us a fuller understanding of ourselves, and of our common humanity, so that we can better face the future."

—Robert Penn Warren, American poet and novelist

The history of each nation is punctuated by momentous events that represent turning points for that nation, with an impact felt far beyond its borders. These events—displaying the full range of human capabilities, from violence, greed, and ignorance to heroism, courage, and strength—are nearly always complicated and multifaceted. Any student of history faces the challenge of grasping the many strands that constitute such world-changing events as wars, social movements, and environmental disasters. But understanding these significant historic events can be enhanced by exposure to a variety of perspectives, whether of people involved intimately or of ones observing from a distance of miles or years. Understanding can also be increased by learning about the controversies surrounding such events and exploring hot-button issues from multiple angles. Finally, true understanding of important historic events involves knowledge of the events' human impact—of the ways such events affected people in their everyday lives—all over the world.

Perspectives on Modern World History examines global historic events from the twentieth-century onward by presenting analysis and observation from numerous vantage points. Each volume offers high school, early college level, and general interest readers a thematically arranged anthology of previously published materials that address a major historical event, with an emphasis on international coverage. Each volume opens with background information on the event, then presents the controversies surrounding that event, and concludes with first-person narratives from people who lived through the event or were affected by it. By providing primary sources from the time of the event, as well as relevant commentary surrounding the event, this series can be used to inform debate, help develop critical thinking skills, increase global awareness, and enhance an understanding of international perspectives on history.

Material in each volume is selected from a diverse range of sources, including journals, magazines, newspapers, nonfiction books, personal narratives, speeches, congressional testimony, government documents, pamphlets, organization newsletters, and position papers Articles taken from these sources are carefully edited and introduced to provide context and background. Each volume of Perspectives on Modern World History includes an array of views on events of global significance. Much of the material comes from international sources and from U.S. sources that provide extensive international coverage.

Each volume in the Perspectives on Modern World History series also includes:

- A full-color **world map**, offering context and geographic perspective.
- An annotated **table of contents** that provides a brief summary of each essay in the volume.
- An **introduction** specific to the volume topic.
- For each viewpoint, a brief **introduction** that has notes about the author and source of the viewpoint, and that provides a summary of its main points.
- Full-color **charts**, **graphs**, **maps**, and other visual representations.

- Informational **sidebars** that explore the lives of key individuals, give background on historical events, or explain scientific or technical concepts.
- A **glossary** that defines key terms, as needed.
- A **chronology** of important dates preceding, during, and immediately following the event.
- A **bibliography** of additional books, periodicals, and Web sites for further research.
- A comprehensive **subject index** that offers access to people, places, and events cited in the text.

Perspectives on Modern World History is designed for a broad spectrum of readers who want to learn more about not only history but also current events, political science, government, international relations, and sociology—students doing research for class assignments or debates, teachers and faculty seeking to supplement course materials, and others wanting to improve their understanding of history. Each volume of Perspectives on Modern World History is designed to illuminate a complicated event, to spark debate, and to show the human perspective behind the world's most significant happenings of recent decades.

INTRODUCTION

It has been nearly half a century since the assassination of President John F. Kennedy. Yet the subject continues to fascinate people not only in the United States but all over the world, and many who were alive when it happened still mourn him. Many more feel that the past decades might have been different if it had not happened. Kennedy soon became, and remains, a symbol of hope unfulfilled.

This is not to say that everyone admired President Kennedy during his lifetime. On the contrary, he was elected by an extremely narrow margin, and although his approval rating after taking office was consistently higher than that of most presidents, it was at its lowest ebb just before he was killed. His visit to Dallas, Texas, where he was shot, was a stop on a reelection campaign trip. What has been written about his assassination emphasizes the overwhelming grief of Americans, but it was not always personal grief; there were many people who were not emotionally stricken but were merely appalled by the fact that the president of the United States had been murdered.

The collective sorrow of the majority overshadowed the less intense feeling of the rest, and the hopes many had for what "might have been" grew more and more prominent as time passed. Would Kennedy have pulled the United States out of Vietnam before the war there escalated? Could he have brought about faster progress on civil rights legislation and disarmament? Could the later assassinations of his brother Robert and of Martin Luther King Jr. have been prevented? Of course, no one can know the answers to these questions.

Most commentators agree, however, that the Kennedy assassination did have a direct effect on Americans' attitudes toward the government and, perhaps, on their own sense of security. Because the question of who was behind the murder has never been conclusively answered, many people are convinced that the government has been withholding information about a conspiracy of some kind. To be sure, conspiracy theories abound on a number of issues related to the government, and it is understood that it must conceal classified information on subjects vital to national security. But the assassination invokes more disturbing feelings. Many people do not want to believe that one deranged assassin acting all by himself—as the government's report of the official investigations says it happened—can eliminate a great leader and thereby change the course of history. If this is true, they reason, then the nation could be at the mercy of any madman with a gun who comes along. Some find it more comfortable to assume that only a powerful group of conspirators could commit such a crime and that, therefore, the government must be lying. On the other hand, the belief that the government lies is not reassuring either. In the light of these conflicting emotions, it is not surprising that distrust of the government has grown since the assassination and that the question of who killed Kennedy remains controversial.

Kennedy had not had time to achieve his goals when his life was cut short. The most widely acknowledged aspect of his influence is the effect he had on the nation's youth. In the December 6, 1999, issue of the *New Statesman* Karl E. Meyer wrote:

> What made the funeral unbearably moving was the uncounted tens of thousands of young people who came from afar as if by invisible command to Washington. At freezing dawn they formed most of a line far more than a mile long of those waiting to pass the President's coffin in the dimly lit dome of the Capitol. Until one stood with them, it was impossible fully to grasp what

President Kennedy meant to the generation for which he spoke.

The United States was then in the midst of the Cold War, and young people at that time had lived since childhood with the fear of nuclear attack. "Duck and cover" air raid drills were common in the schools. The building of backyard fallout shelters was advocated. Kennedy encouraged these tactics but at the same time offered hope that they would not always be necessary. He brought about a resolution of the Cuban missile crisis, an incident in October 1962 during which the nation came closer to war than the public then realized, by convincing the Soviet Union to remove nuclear missiles aimed at the U.S. that it had placed in Cuba. The next year, he succeeded in negotiating a treaty banning nuclear tests in the atmosphere. Young people, lacking experience with past attempts to end the threat of war, felt that he might really manage to do it.

Kennedy also inspired young people with his famous inaugural speech in which he urged, "Ask not what your country can do for you; ask what you can do for your country." He established the Peace Corps, a program in which volunteers serve as teachers and technical assistants to the people of undeveloped nations. He was a strong supporter of rights for black Americans, and at the time of his death was attempting to get a civil rights bill through Congress. All of these elements contributed to the perception of the "new frontier" he promised, which was embodied in the metaphor of Camelot—the idealized kingdom of Arthurian legend—that was applied to his presidency after his death.

One of President Kennedy's most significant acts was his decision to send Americans to the moon. Before a joint session of Congress on May 25, 1961, he said, "Now it is time to take longer strides—time for this nation to take a clearly leading role in space achievement, which in many ways may hold the key to our future on Earth. . . . I believe that this nation should commit itself to achieving the goal, before this decade is out, of landing a man on the Moon and returning him safely to the Earth. No single space project . . . will be more exciting, or more impressive to mankind, or more important . . . and none will be so difficult or expensive to accomplish." In view of the lack of commitment to space exploration that has existed since the success of the Apollo moon landings, the importance of his personal endorsement of that goal is plain, and some people believe that historians of future centuries will consider it his greatest achievement.

In an article in the December 6, 1983, issue of *Life* magazine, Theodore H. White recorded Jacqueline Kennedy's comments on her late husband's interest in space. "She remembered that in every speech in their last days in Texas, he had spoken of how in December this nation would loft the largest rocket booster yet into the sky, making us first in space. So she had wanted something of his there when it went up—perhaps only his initials painted on a tiny corner of the great Saturn, where no one would even notice it. But now Americans will seek the moon from Cape Kennedy." The renaming of Cape Canaveral took place shortly after the assassination, and though ten years later its original name was restored, the NASA launch facilities there still carry the name Kennedy Space Center—a fitting memorial to the president whose farsightedness led to humankind's first steps on another world.

On the whole, however, Kennedy is remembered not as much for the things he achieved as for what he might have achieved if he had lived. "Dallas put an end to JFK, the Man," wrote Joe Sherlock in his blog "The View from the Windshield" on November 22, 2004. "His promise was unfulfilled, his administration unfinished. But JFK, the Legend, was born on that November afternoon." The prevalent vision of the future that was lost is rosier than the reality that would probably have developed, for no one can be wholly successful in bringing all of his or her hopes for the world to fruition. Yet even people who expected little good from his presidency, those who might have voted against his reelection, grieve over the effect his passing had on the nation.

On the fortieth anniversary of Kennedy's assassination Cal Thomas wrote in *Jewish World Review*, "For some, all things seemed possible with Kennedy in the White House. When he died, most things seemed impossible. There was a sense we had been robbed of hope, and hope denied produces cynicism and despair." Certainly cynicism took hold in the late sixties, as well as the distrust of government that had not existed before; it has become a truism that Kennedy's death marked the loss of Americans' innocence. Much more contributed to this shift than the assassination and suspicions of a government conspiracy alone, but most observers feel they were a major factor in it.

Thomas went on to say of Kennedy, "Speaking as one who became a conservative and realizes that the 'myth' of Camelot was exactly that, I still miss him. Even more, I miss much that was good in American life that seems to have perished with him."

But the values he has come to symbolize have not perished. People not yet born when Kennedy died are still inspired by those values and will honor his memory for a long time to come.

World Map

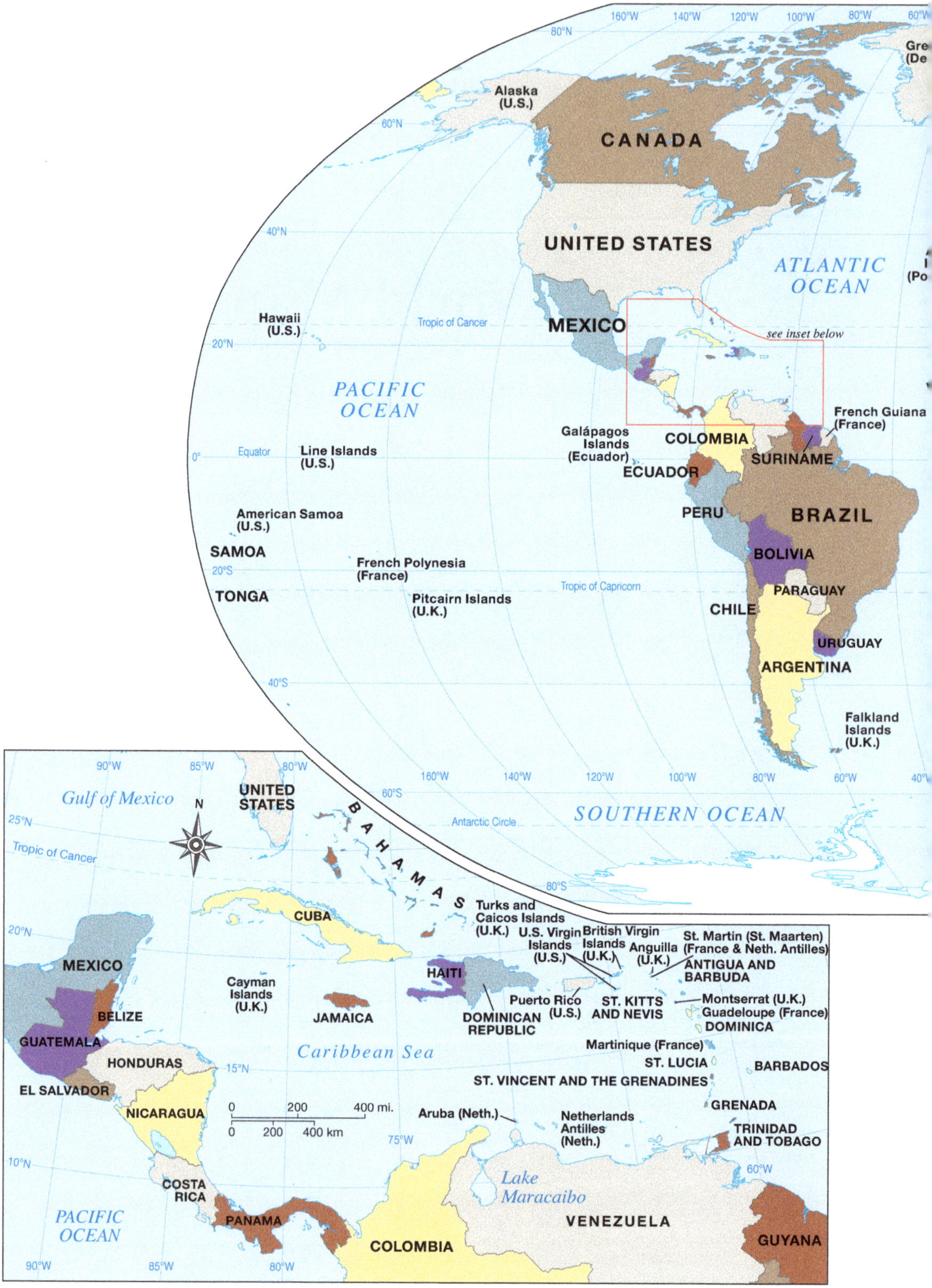

Alaska (U.S.)
CANADA
UNITED STATES
ATLANTIC OCEAN
MEXICO
Hawaii (U.S.)
Tropic of Cancer
see inset below
PACIFIC OCEAN
French Guiana (France)
Galápagos Islands (Ecuador)
COLOMBIA
Equator
Line Islands (U.S.)
SURINAME
ECUADOR
American Samoa (U.S.)
PERU
BRAZIL
SAMOA
BOLIVIA
French Polynesia (France)
Tropic of Capricorn
TONGA
Pitcairn Islands (U.K.)
PARAGUAY
CHILE
URUGUAY
ARGENTINA
Falkland Islands (U.K.)
SOUTHERN OCEAN
Antarctic Circle
160°W
140°W
120°W
100°W
80°W
60°W
80°N
60°N
40°N
20°N
0°
20°S
40°S
60°S
80°S
Gulf of Mexico
UNITED STATES
BAHAMAS
Tropic of Cancer
CUBA
Turks and Caicos Islands (U.K.)
U.S. Virgin Islands (U.S.)
British Virgin Islands (U.K.)
Anguilla (U.K.)
St. Martin (St. Maarten) (France & Neth. Antilles)
ANTIGUA AND BARBUDA
MEXICO
HAITI
Cayman Islands (U.K.)
Puerto Rico (U.S.)
ST. KITTS AND NEVIS
Montserrat (U.K.)
Guadeloupe (France)
BELIZE
JAMAICA
DOMINICAN REPUBLIC
DOMINICA
GUATEMALA
Caribbean Sea
Martinique (France)
HONDURAS
ST. LUCIA
BARBADOS
EL SALVADOR
ST. VINCENT AND THE GRENADINES
0 200 400 mi.
0 200 400 km
GRENADA
NICARAGUA
Aruba (Neth.)
Netherlands Antilles (Neth.)
TRINIDAD AND TOBAGO
COSTA RICA
Lake Maracaibo
PACIFIC OCEAN
PANAMA
VENEZUELA
GUYANA
COLOMBIA
90°W
85°W
80°W
75°W
60°W
25°N
20°N
15°N
10°N
N

0°
20°E
40°E
60°E
80°E
100°E
120°E
140°E
160°E
80°N
TIC OCEAN
see inset below
ctic Circle
RUSSIA
60°N
KAZAKHSTAN
MONGOLIA
GEORGIA
AZER.
ARMENIA
UZBEK.
TURKMEN.
KYRGYZSTAN
TAJIKISTAN
NORTH KOREA
SOUTH KOREA
JAPAN
40°N
CHINA
PACIFIC OCEAN
IRAQ
IRAN
AFGHAN.
ISRAEL
JORDAN
KUWAIT
BAHRAIN
QATAR
PAKISTAN
NEPAL
BHUTAN
ALGERIA
LIBYA
EGYPT
SAUDI ARABIA
U.A.E.
OMAN
INDIA
MYANMAR (BURMA)
BANGLADESH
LAOS
TAIWAN (Claimed by China)
20°N
CHAD
SUDAN
ERITREA
YEMEN
DJIBOUTI
ETHIOPIA
THAILAND
VIETNAM
CAMBODIA
PHILIPPINES
MARSHALL ISLANDS
CEN. AFR. REP.
CAMEROON
SRI LANKA
BRUNEI
MALAYSIA
SOMALIA
MALDIVES
FEDERATED STATES OF MICRONESIA
KIRIBATI
DEM. REP. OF THE CONGO
UGANDA
KENYA
RWANDA
BURUNDI
GABON
CONGO
SÃO TOMÉ PRÍNCIPE
SINGAPORE
INDONESIA
NAURU
PAPUA NEW GUINEA
SOLOMON ISLANDS
0°
TANZANIA
SEYCHELLES
INDIAN OCEAN
TIMOR-LESTE
TUVALU
NTIC EAN
ANGOLA
MALAWI
ZAMBIA
COMOROS
MOZAMBIQUE
FIJI ISLANDS
VANUATU
MADAGASCAR
MAURITIUS
ZIMBABWE
BOTSWANA
NAMIBIA
Réunion (France)
20°S
AUSTRALIA
New Caledonia (France)
SOUTH AFRICA
SWAZILAND
LESOTHO
0 1000 2000 mi.
0 1000 2000 km
N
NEW ZEALAND
40°S
40°E
60°E
80°E
100°E
120°E
140°E
160°E
60°S
SOUTHERN OCEAN
0°
20°E
ANTARCTICA

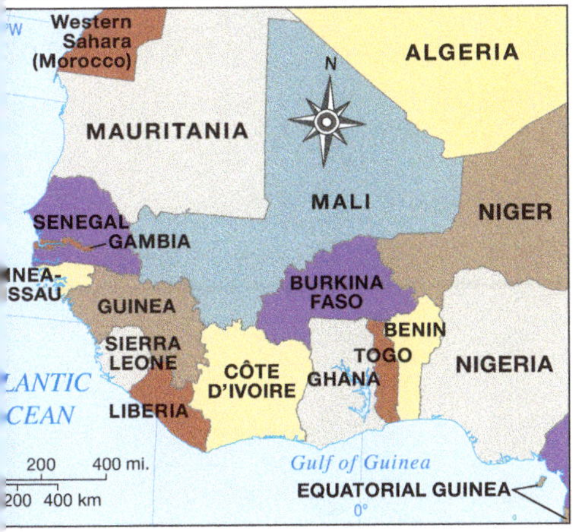

Western Sahara (Morocco)
ALGERIA
N
MAURITANIA
MALI
NIGER
SENEGAL
GAMBIA
INEA-SSAU
GUINEA
BURKINA FASO
BENIN
SIERRA LEONE
TOGO
NIGERIA
CÔTE D'IVOIRE
GHANA
LANTIC CEAN
LIBERIA
200 400 mi.
200 400 km
Gulf of Guinea
EQUATORIAL GUINEA
0°

50°E
70°N
N
SWEDEN
FINLAND
NORWAY
0 200 400 mi.
0 200 400 km
ESTONIA
North Sea
DENMARK
Baltic Sea
LATVIA
RUSSIA
IRELAND
UNITED KINGDOM
LITHUANIA
RUSSIA
NETHERLANDS
BELARUS
POLAND
ATLANTIC OCEAN
GERMANY
BELGIUM
LUX.
CZECH REP.
UKRAINE
LIECH.
SLOVAKIA
Bay of Biscay
FRANCE
SWITZ.
AUSTRIA
MOLDOVA
HUNGARY
SLOVENIA
ROMANIA
CROATIA
ANDORRA
MONACO
ITALY
BOS. AND HERZ.
SERBIA
PORTUGAL
SAN MARINO
Black Sea
Corsica (France)
MONT.
BULGARIA
SPAIN
MAC.
Sardinia (Italy)
VATICAN CITY
ALBANIA
TURKEY
Gibraltar (U.K.)
Balearic Isands (Spain)
GREECE
Ceuta (Spain)
Melilla (Spain)
Sicily (Italy)
MALTA
Mediterranean Sea
CYPRUS
SYRIA
MOROCCO
ALGERIA
TUNISIA
Crete (Greece)
LEBANON

CHAPTER 1

Historical Background on the Assassination of John F. Kennedy

VIEWPOINT 1

An Overview of the Kennedy Assassination

Crime and Punishment: Essential Primary Sources

On November 22, 1963, President John F. Kennedy was shot and killed while riding through Dallas, Texas, in a motorcade. Not only Americans, but people all over the world, were deeply grieved by his death. The assassin, Lee Harvey Oswald, was himself murdered by a minor underworld figure shortly after his arrest, resulting in a widespread belief that there must have been a conspiracy. This belief has persisted over the years despite the official conclusion that Oswald acted alone and was intensified by the 1991 movie *JFK*, which led to declassification of thousands of government documents related to the case but uncovered no new evidence. More than one thousand books have been written about the assassination, but no proof that it was the work of a conspiracy has ever been produced.

Photo on previous page: President John F. Kennedy was assassinated November 22, 1963, as he rode through the streets of Dallas, Texas. **(AP Images.)**

SOURCE. *Crime and Punishment: Essential Primary Sources.* Belmont, CA: Gale, 2006.

At 12:30 P.M. on November 22, 1963, while driving through downtown Dallas, Texas, in a motorcade, John F. Kennedy, the thirty-fifth President of the United States, was shot by a lone gunman firing from the window of a nearby building. He was hit four times and declared dead at Parkland Hospital one hour later. Texas Governor, John Connally, who was riding in the front of the Kennedy car, was also shot and seriously wounded, but survived.

Kennedy was the fourth American president to be assassinated and the eighth to die in office. Vice President Lyndon B. Johnson, who had been driving in the same motorcade but a different car, was sworn in as president at 2:38 P.M. on Air Force One as it flew back to Washington, D.C., with President Kennedy's body.

It was not only the most notorious murder in twentieth century American history, but also the most investigated.

The assassination of John F. Kennedy sent the western world into a period of collective mourning. It was not only the most notorious murder in twentieth century American history, but also the most investigated. The notion of a "JFK moment"—i.e., where an individual was when he or she heard the astonishing news—became engrained in popular culture. When Kennedy's assassin, Lee Harvey Oswald, was himself murdered less than forty-eight hours after his arrest, a multitude of conspiracy theories arose, which still abound four decades later.

Lee Harvey Oswald

Oswald, a twenty-four-year-old former Marine who had spent time in the USSR, was arrested hours after Kennedy's assassination after shooting and killing a police officer. The ten-month-long investigation into Kennedy's murder by the Warren Commission concluded in 1964 that Oswald—and Oswald alone—carried out the shooting. Evidence given to the Commission painted a portrait of a wife-beating tyrant with delusions of grandeur. He had failed at everything he had attempted in life—military career, a professional life, a flirtation with Marxism—except, it seemed, the murder of the President of the United States.

Oswald's reasons for carrying out the killing went with him to his grave. Oswald was himself shot dead on November 24, 1963, by Jack Ruby, a minor figure in the Dallas underworld, who had lunged from a crowd of journalists and police at the police department building where Oswald was being held. Unable to elicit Oswald's testimony, the Warren Commission [the commission established to investigate Kennedy's assassination] concluded that it could not "ascribe to him any one motive or group of motives." However, it went on to state that "Oswald was moved by an overriding hostility to his environment."

A quotation from an October 2, 1964, *Time* magazine article sums up Oswald in these terms:

> He does not appear to have been able to establish meaningful relationships with other people. He was perpetually discontented with the world around him. Long before the assassination he expressed his hatred for American society and acted in protest against it. Oswald's search for what he conceived to be the perfect society was doomed from the start. He sought for himself a place in history—a role as the "great man" who would be recognized as having been in advance of his times. His commitment to Marxism and communism appears to have been another important factor in his motivation. He also had demonstrated [through the attempt to kill General Walker] a capacity to act decisively and without regard to the consequences when such action would further his aims of the moment. Out of these and the many other factors which may have molded the character of

Lee Harvey Oswald there emerged a man capable of assassinating President Kennedy.

The Rise of Conspiracy Theories

Yet Oswald's death before he could stand trial and his murder by a shady figure like Ruby gave rise to a multitude of conspiracy theories, many of which were originally dealt with and dismissed by the Warren Commission. Nevertheless, these theories continued to re-emerge over subsequent decades. The idea that Kennedy was murdered on the instructions of some greater force was given credence in 1979 by a House Select Committee on Assassinations, which directly contradicted the Warren Commission. Using acoustic evidence it concluded that Oswald "probably did not act on his own" and that a second gunman was operating from a grassy knoll. It claimed that Kennedy was probably killed as the result of a conspiracy. In addition, it said it did not know who might have conspired with Oswald in the shooting, but it specifically excluded many of the usual scapegoats, including the FBI, the CIA, the Secret Service, the Soviet

Investigators removed this rifle from the Texas School Book Depository in Dallas after the shooting; authorities consider it the weapon that killed President Kennedy. **(Terry Ashe/Time Life Pictures/Getty Images.)**

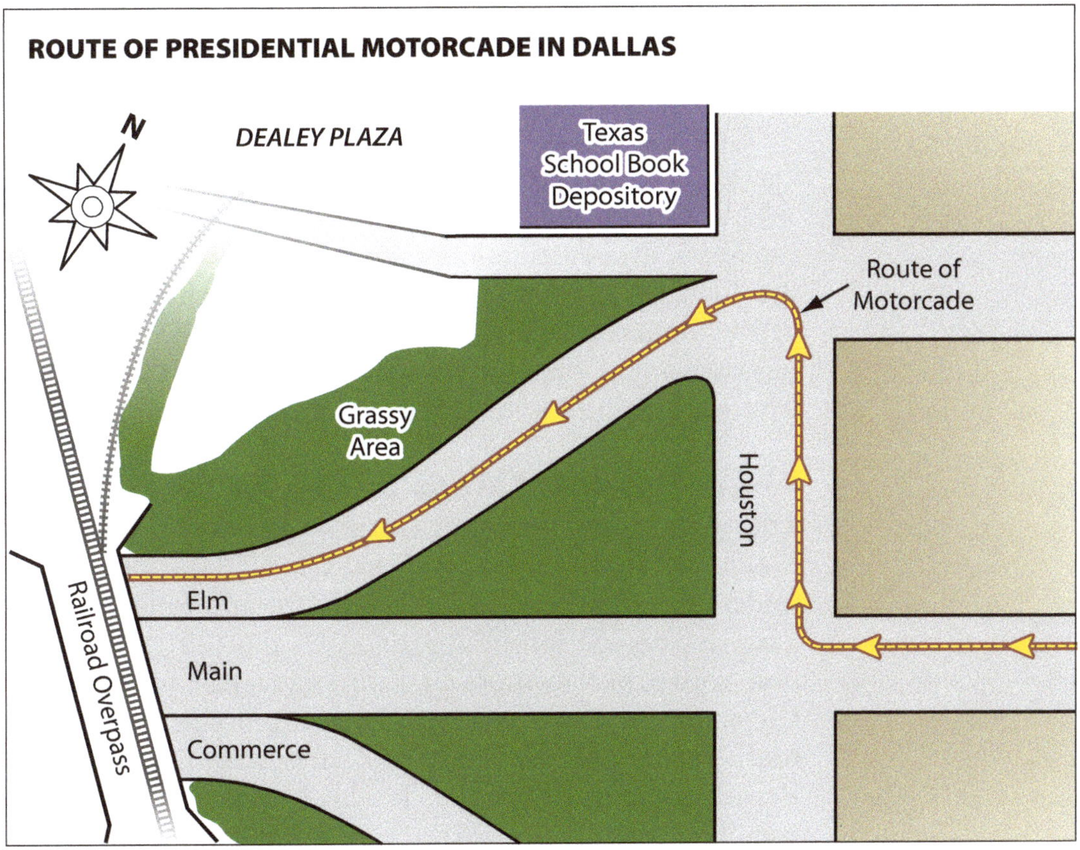

government, the Cuban government, anti-Castro Cuban groups, and the Mafia.

The 1991 Oliver Stone movie *JFK* engendered a renewed interest in the case. The movie, which its critics claimed was replete with historical inaccuracies and half truths, followed the story of New Orleans district attorney Jim Garrison, who in the late 1960s prosecuted the only Kennedy case that ever went to trial. Garrison had claimed a vast plot involving homosexual intrigue, the U.S. military-industrial complex, and Fidel Castro, but after thirty-four days of evidence, the jury threw the case out after less than a day of deliberations, finding the defendant, businessman Clay Shaw, not guilty. Following the release of the film, the U.S. government took the unprecedented step of declassifying thousands of documents pertaining to the case. None of these documents pointed to anything other than what the Warren Commission had found thirty years earlier—that Lee Harvey Oswald alone killed President Kennedy.

More than 1,000 books have been published about the Kennedy assassination, many of which also question the findings of the Warren Commission that Oswald acted alone. Unlike the 1979 House Select Committee on Assassinations, many draw their own conclusions as to who was behind Kennedy's assassination.

Alleged Involvement of the Mafia

The two principal conspiracy theories center on America's Mafia. The first variation was that Oswald was operating under the instructions of Fidel Castro and killed Kennedy as revenge for an abortive CIA plot—in conjunction with Chicago mobster Sam Giancana—to kill the Cuban leader. The second revolved around the American Mafia's sense of betrayal by the Kennedy administration. President Kennedy's father, Joseph Kennedy, had long-standing connections with the Mob that dated back to his time as a Prohibition-era bootlegger. During his son's run for president in 1960 he had called in numerous favors, not least in Illinois where widespread ballot stuffing and other electoral fraud carried out by local Mafiosi had helped secure a narrow and crucial Democratic victory. Mobsters who had hopes for an easy time under the Kennedy presidency soon were disappointed with the appointment of the president's brother, Robert, as Attorney General. Under his leadership, the U.S. Justice Department waged a war against organized crime, indicting 116 members of the Mob. According

> "Despite the glut of conspiracy theories and accompanying literature, firm evidence linking some wider plot to the murder of President Kennedy has never been forthcoming."

to those who perpetuate this theory, the president's assassination was carried out by the Mafia as retribution for promises of immunity—made in return for favors in vote-rigging key states—that were betrayed once he became president. Jack Ruby then murdered Oswald to silence him.

Yet, despite the glut of conspiracy theories and accompanying literature, firm evidence linking some wider plot to the murder of President Kennedy has never been forthcoming. Nevertheless, America remains unconvinced. Even forty years after President Kennedy's death, opinion polls still regularly find that only between one in five and one in three Americans believe Oswald acted alone. As long as books continue to be written about this case, such speculation and uncertainty will almost certainly continue.

What John F. Kennedy Meant to Americans

Carl M. Brauer

John F. Kennedy meant a great deal to Americans because of what he represented: youth, hope, and idealism. The following excerpt from a short biography tells a little about Kennedy's background and the accomplishments for which he is best known. Years after his death, he was rated best of the nine most recent presidents, although he was elected by a narrow margin and his popularity was at its lowest point just before his assassination. His greatest strength lay in his ability to inspire people. It was hoped that he could make progress toward ending the Cold War, and ever since his death many have wondered whether he might have been able to do so. Carl M. Brauer, an American historian and biographer, is the author of many books, articles, and reference works.

SOURCE. Carl M. Brauer, *The Presidents: A Reference History*. Belmont, CA: Charles Scribners Sons, 2002.

Twenty years after John F. Kennedy was assassinated, a public opinion poll indicated that he was rated best overall of the nine presidents since Herbert Hoover. Among five positive attributes surveyed, Kennedy "most inspired confidence in the White House," according to 40 percent of those asked, followed by Franklin D. Roosevelt at 23 percent. Sixty percent considered Kennedy as having had the "most appealing personality," followed again by Roosevelt at 11 percent. Kennedy edged Roosevelt on "best in domestic affairs" and on having "cared most about the elderly, the poor and those most in economic trouble." Political scientists, historians, and national journalists have on the whole tended to view Kennedy less favorably than has the general public. Some "experts" hold Kennedy in high regard, but others are extremely critical of him. A significant number probably agree that his promise outstripped his performance and that he left an ambiguous legacy.

> Kennedy's place in history revolves around unanswerable questions of what might have been had he lived.

Neither popular nor expert opinion would actually be wrong about Kennedy. Indeed, they are in a sense opposite sides of the same coin, for Kennedy's inflation to mythic proportions by the public and his demythologizing by experts both derive significantly from the manner of his death. No one knows how his reputation might have been affected had he served out his first term and the second term to which he likely would have been elected. Alone among modern presidents, Kennedy's place in history revolves around unanswerable questions of what might have been had he lived. Yet this very fact suggests that in his relatively brief presidency—less than three years—Kennedy exerted a profound influence upon both popular and expert hopes and expectations, which endured long after his death. Had Kennedy not had this influence while he lived, the public would not have mythologized him, nor the experts demythologized him, after he was killed. Had he not had this influence, his successors in the White House would have been far less likely to have compared themselves to him, to have sought to emulate him, or to have tried to escape his myth.

Family Background

John F. Kennedy was born on 29 May 1917 in Brookline, Massachusetts, the second son of Joseph P. Kennedy, a self-made multimillionaire. . . .

Jack, as he was known, grew up in a home where political issues were frequently discussed and sometimes debated. His father's strong views evidently influenced his older brother, Joseph P. Kennedy, Jr., more than they did him. All the Kennedy children, but particularly the four boys—Joseph, John, Robert, and Edward—were brought up with a strong sense of noblesse oblige and with little or no interest in enhancing their own very considerable financial fortunes. (Their father set up trust funds for each of them, which made them financially independent when they reached maturity.) Public service, not private gain, was the ideal instilled in all the Kennedy children. When their private fortunes or family connections could enhance their ability to perform public service, as in getting their views known or in winning elections, for example, the Kennedy boys gladly used them.

Jack Kennedy was a sickly child and adolescent. . . . During his illnesses, he became an avid reader and also a fatalist. He never let his frail condition keep him from throwing himself headlong into his family's fierce athletic competitions. At Choate, a predominantly Protestant boarding school in Connecticut, he was an average student, though one who, his teachers believed, performed at less than his potential. His peers liked him for his wit and cleverness, and he proved adept at winning

The First Family

One of the reasons the public was emotionally attached to President John F. Kennedy was that, unlike former presidents who were much older, he had a young family that represented what many viewed as the American ideal. His attractive and talented wife, Jacqueline Kennedy—one of the youngest first ladies in history—was greatly admired not only by Americans but by the foreign dignitaries she entertained on state visits or met on overseas trips. She was interested in the fine arts and brought cultural events to the White House, as well as redecorating it with furnishings of historical significance. The clothes she wore set styles for women all over the world.

The Kennedy children, Caroline (who turned six just after the assassination) and John Jr., often called John-John (whose third birthday came the day of the funeral), were the subject of wide public interest, although Jacqueline tried to preserve their privacy. A third child, Patrick, had been born prematurely three months earlier, but had lived only a few days because of undeveloped lungs. Jacqueline had not yet fully recovered from that tragedy at the time of her husband's murder.

Affectionately referred to by the media as Jack and Jackie, the couple was generally thought to have a perfect marriage. In later years it was learned that this was not true. In fact, Jack Kennedy was involved with many women before and during his years in the White House. But in that era the private lives of public figures were not as minutely investigated by news reporters as they are today, and Americans had every reason to believe in and be inspired by the prevailing image of the First Family.

friends. He was admired not for his accomplishments, a teacher later observed, but for his personality. . . .

In college, Kennedy for the most part showed a greater dedication to enjoying himself socially than he did to developing his mind. Once again he was popular and made lasting friends. Once again he suffered from impaired health, including a back injury sustained in playing football. Although he had suffered from backaches even as a child, this injury probably marked the beginning of a chronically bad back. . . .

During the war, Kennedy commanded a PT boat in the South Pacific. While on patrol one night, the small boat was cut in half by a Japanese destroyer traveling at high speed. Two of the crewmen were killed. Kennedy demonstrated leadership, courage, and stamina in helping to save the eleven survivors. . . .

Early Career

John Kennedy began to make speeches around Massachusetts in 1945 and the following spring ran in a primary for a vacant congressional seat in Boston, where nomination was tantamount to election. Although only twenty-nine, he had an impressive war record, his father's financial assistance and personal connections, and excellent name recognition. . . . Youthful-looking and handsome, though gaunt and often on crutches, Kennedy proved a tireless campaigner and showed a deft touch in greeting the Irish politicians and working people whose support he needed. His campaign stressed the bread-and-butter needs of his constituents and of the returning veterans. He won the primary impressively and then the general election.

In 1952, Kennedy captured the Senate seat held by Henry Cabot Lodge, Jr. . . .

In 1953, Kennedy married Jacqueline Bouvier, a beautiful socialite twelve years his junior. After he died, books and articles eventually made the claim, never confirmed by his widow, that their marriage was not happy, that it suffered under the strains of his infidelities and her lavish spending and unease with politics. During his life, they made an extraordinarily attractive couple, with the aura of royalty about them. Rumors of marital difficulties were not widely circulated. If the public was shown less than a completely honest picture of their marriage, that was not an unusual practice in American politics. Neither was it out of the ordinary for a politician to be less than candid about health problems, which in Kennedy's case were much more serious than was publicly acknowledged. But personal adversities, whatever they might have been, failed to impede his energetic pursuit of high office.

While convalescing from back surgery in 1955, Kennedy conceived of a book about political courage. Published in early 1956, *Profiles in Courage* described historical instances of senators placing the national interest above parochial or self-interest. A front-page review in the *New York Times Book Review* hailed the book for restoring "respect for a venerable and much abused profession," politics. The book became a best-seller and won a Pulitzer Prize. More important, it established Kennedy as that American rarity, an intellectual politician, and identified him with political courage. . . .

Presidential Campaign

The 1960 presidential campaign came against an ambiguous background. The country was at peace and there was general prosperity. [Dwight D.] Eisenhower remained a popular president who, even Kennedy partisans agree, could have been reelected to a third term had not the recently enacted Twenty-second Amendment prohibited it. Yet a series of events, disclosures, and reports suggested that the United States was slipping in its decade-long struggle to contain Communism. The Soviet Union, it appeared, was moving ahead of the

United States in winning friends in the new, decolonized nations of the world; was making rapid strides in science and technology, as evidenced by its launching of *Sputnik* [the first Earth-orbiting satellite]; and was besting America in weapons development, presumably causing a "missile gap." At home, a popular argument went, Americans were sated with consumer goods and insufficiently committed to public needs in such areas as job development and economic growth, education, medical care, and civil rights for the nation's black minority. Eisenhower, however popular he remained, seemed to influential opinion leaders, if not to the general public, a passive observer of America's deterioration.

> Kennedy transformed himself from a president-elect without a clear mandate to a highly popular incumbent who raised public expectations of the office.

Kennedy ran on the slogans "Get America Moving Again" and "To Seek a New Frontier." . . .

The election was so close that any one of a variety of different groups and tactics may be said to have determined the outcome. With a popular vote of 34.2 million, Kennedy won by fewer than 120,000 votes out of nearly 70 million cast. His margin in the Electoral College, 303–219, was more comfortable, yet it rested on thin majorities in a dozen states. Had fewer than 12,000 people in five states switched their votes, [Richard] Nixon would have had an electoral majority. . . .

Decisive Leadership

Within the space of a few months, Kennedy transformed himself from a president-elect without a clear mandate to a highly popular incumbent who raised public expectations of the office. The most visible moment in this transformation came with his inauguration itself, where the contrast between him and Eisenhower could not have been more striking. Eisenhower was the oldest man to occupy the presidency until that time; Kennedy, at forty-three, was the youngest person ever elected president. Eisenhower was the last president born in the nineteenth century; Kennedy was the first born in the twentieth. . . .

Kennedy's inaugural address vividly underscored the changing of the guard, while promising to uphold America's commitments:

> Let the word go forth from this time and place, to friend and foe alike, that the torch has been passed to a new generation of Americans, born in this century, tempered by war, disciplined by a hard and bitter peace, proud of our ancient heritage, and unwilling to witness or permit the slow undoing of those human rights to which this nation has always been committed, and to which we are committed today at home and around the world.

It was one of the shortest inaugural addresses of this century and the most effective and memorable since Franklin D. Roosevelt's in 1933. Delivered on a cold, clear day following a heavy snowstorm, it would always be remembered by those in attendance and the many millions more who watched it on television or heard it on radio. Young people were particularly stirred by its idealism and inspired by the young man who delivered it so crisply and self-confidently. In the speech's famous climax, Kennedy declared:

> In the long history of the world, only a few generations have been granted the role of defending freedom in its hour of maximum danger. I do not shrink from this responsibility; I welcome it. I do not believe that any of us would exchange places with any other people or any other generation. The energy, the faith, the devotion which we bring to this endeavor will light our country and all who serve it, and the glow from the fire can truly light the world.

> And so, my fellow Americans, ask not what your country can do for you; ask what you can do for your country.
>
> My fellow citizens of the world, ask not what America will do for you, but what together we can do for the freedom of man. . . .

Kennedy . . . encouraged social criticism, and he generated interest in politics and public service. During his presidency, the numbers and impact of published critiques of social conditions and injustices increased appreciably. The Peace Corps, which he created by executive order on 1 March 1961, tapped the idealism of thousands of Americans, many of them young, who volunteered to go to poor countries as teachers, health-care providers, and technicians, and to fulfill other scarce needs. Under Kennedy's direct inspiration, many young people embarked on careers in government and politics, which Kennedy gave a respectability and appeal they had usually lacked. . . .

"The Peace Corps, which [Kennedy] created by executive order on 1 March 1961, tapped the idealism of thousands of Americans, many of them young."

The Cuban Missile Crisis

Ever since [Prime Minister Fidel] Castro's Communist sympathies had become clear, Cuba had been a sore point in American politics, for Americans were uncomfortable with a Communist government so close at hand. . . .

When, in mid-October [1962], Kennedy received incontrovertible photographic evidence that the Soviets were building launching sites [in Cuba] for intermediate-range missiles, he simply had to stop them. . . .

More important to Kennedy than technical military considerations were political ones, both international

Photo on opposite page: His youth and vigor made President John F. Kennedy a dashing embodiment of hope for a better American future—a new frontier, as it was called. **(AP Images.)**

and domestic. Kennedy had to worry about how the Soviets might interpret a capitulation by him on this issue. If they had miscalculated this badly on missiles in Cuba, would they next miscalculate on Berlin [during this time tensions increased regarding the fate of West Berlin], for example, where he would not back down, with the result a nuclear war? If Kennedy did nothing about the missiles, moreover, his political position in the United States would be compromised or destroyed. . . .

On 21 October he proceeded to announce the imposition of a naval blockade, which he called a quarantine, in a crisp and carefully worded television speech.

The crisis was joined, and the world held its breath to see what the Soviets would do. . . . Kennedy and [Soviet premier Nikita] Khrushchev communicated privately by cable and through emissaries. In these communications, Kennedy demonstrated considerable skill and forbearance, ignoring a tough message from Khrushchev and responding to a more conciliatory one. . . . On 28 October, Khrushchev relented and began removal of the missiles. The crisis passed. . . .

The crisis impelled Kennedy to take new initiatives in seeking an end to the Cold War. At American University on 10 June 1963, he gave one of the most important speeches of his presidency; it marked the beginning of a spirit of détente [a relaxation of tensions]. Kennedy called for a reexamination of American attitudes toward the Soviet Union and said that both sides in the Cold War had "a mutually deep interest in a just and genuine peace and in halting the arms race." He declared:

> In the final analysis, our most basic common link is that we all inhabit this small planet. We all breathe the same air. We all cherish our children's future. And we are all mortal. . . . We must deal with the world as it is, and not as it might have been had the history of the last eighteen years been different.

He proposed complete disarmament, to be achieved through stages, the first of which would be a ban on atmospheric nuclear tests. As a demonstration of good faith, he promised that the United States would not conduct any further atmospheric tests as long as other countries refrained from doing so. . . .

Negotiations proved successful, at least in banning atmospheric, though not underground, tests. In August, Kennedy sent the treaty to the Senate; it was the first arms control agreement between Washington and Moscow. . . . The treaty was ratified on 24 September by a comfortable margin above the required two-thirds. It was only a small step toward disarmament and an end to the Cold War, but Kennedy liked to say that great journeys began with small steps. No other accomplishment gave him greater satisfaction.

The Assassination

On 22 November 1963 the world was stunned to learn that Kennedy had been shot to death as he rode in a motorcade in Dallas, Texas. . . . Articles and books about the crime number in the thousands and range from careful and thoughtful investigation and analysis to unsupported speculation and maudlin fantasy. On one level, the fascination with the assassination may indicate a psychological denial of Kennedy's death, a mass wish somehow to make it explicable or, in a sense, to undo it.

> It is probably safe to say that even if Kennedy had died suddenly of natural causes or through an accident, the public grief would have been great.

The depth of the public reaction to Kennedy's assassination can be explained in several ways. Although there had been attempts on the lives of President-elect Franklin D. Roosevelt and President Harry Truman, no American president had been assassinated since William McKinley in 1901. Television brought the

Kennedy tragedy into people's lives with an intimacy that had never been known before. Many thousands had stood by the tracks as Lincoln's funeral train passed by, but now the entire country mourned at a presidential funeral. But it is probably safe to say that even if Kennedy had died suddenly of natural causes or through an accident, the public grief would have been great. Kennedy had become identified with many of mankind's hopes and aspirations—peace, racial justice, economic development, public service, social reform, a striving for excellence, and a seeking after New Frontiers on earth and in space. Toward these goals, he brought vitality, grace, and reason. Then, unexpectedly, irrationally, at the age of forty-six, he was dead, and the world was left wondering what might have been. His death at an early age called up the unfairness and tragedy of life.

VIEWPOINT 3

What It Was Like to Witness the Assassination

Merriman Smith

The following eyewitness story was written by the reporter who conveyed the first news of the attack on President Kennedy. It appeared in many newspapers in the days after the assassination. Merriman Smith was riding several cars behind Kennedy's in the motorcade through Dallas, Texas, and followed the president's car to the hospital. He was there for the announcement of death and then witnessed President Lyndon B. Johnson's swearing-in as the only news service reporter aboard the plane back to Washington, D.C. Merriman Smith was a longtime White House reporter for UPI (United Press International). He won a Pulitzer Prize for his coverage of the Kennedy assassination.

SOURCE. Merriman Smith, "Eyewitness Account of Kennedy Assassination," *Los Angeles Times*, November 23, 1963.

It was a balmy, sunny noon as we followed President Kennedy's car through downtown Dallas. Then, suddenly, we heard three almost painfully loud cracks.

The first sounded as if it might have been a large firecracker. But the second and third were unmistakably gunfire.

Aboard Air Force One shortly after Kennedy's murder, Vice President Lyndon Johnson took the oath of office to become the U.S. president on November 22, 1963. **(Cecil Stoughton/AFP/Getty Images.)**

I was riding in the White House press "pool" car, equipped with a radio-telephone. I was in the front seat between a telephone company driver and Malcolm Kilduff, acting White House press secretary. Three other pool reporters were wedged in the back seat.

As we heard the shots, the President's car, possibly as much as 150 or 200 yards ahead, seemed to falter. There

was a flurry of activity in the Secret Service car behind the President's open limousine.

Flash of Pink

Our car stopped for probably only a few seconds, but it seemed like a lifetime. Even for a trained observer there is a limit to what one can comprehend.

I could not see the President or Gov. John Connally of Texas in their car. I thought I saw a flash of pink, which would have been Mrs. Kennedy.

Everybody in our car began shouting at the driver to pull up closer to the President's car. But at this moment, we saw the limousine and a motorcycle escort roar away at high speed.

We careened around Vice President Lyndon Johnson's car and its escort and set out down the highway, barely able to keep in sight of the President's car.

Lay Face Down

We cleared a curve and saw Parkland Hospital, a large brick structure to the left of the highway. We spilled out of the pool car as it entered the hospital driveway.

I ran to the side of the limousine.

The President lay face down on the back seat. Mrs. Kennedy made a cradle of her arms around the President's head and bent over him as if she were whispering to him.

> "The President lay face down on the back seat. Mrs. Kennedy made a cradle of her arms around the President's head and bent over him."

Gov. Connally was on his back on the floor of the car, his head and shoulders resting in the arms of his wife, Nellie, who kept shaking her head and shaking with dry sobs.

Clint Hill, the Secret Service agent in charge of the detail assigned to Mrs. Kennedy, was leaning over into the rear of the car.

"How badly was he hit, Clint?" I asked.

"He's dead," Hill replied curtly.

I have no further clear memory of the scene in the driveway. I recall a babble of anxious voices, tense voices—"Where in hell are the stretchers . . . get a doctor out here . . . he's on the way . . . come on, easy there." And from somewhere, nervous sobbing.

I raced down a short stretch of sidewalk into a hospital corridor. The first thing I spotted was a small clerical office. Inside a bespectacled man stood shuffling what appeared to be hospital forms. I spotted a telephone on the shelf.

Dictated Bulletin

It took two shaky tries before I successfully dialed the Dallas UPI number. I dictated a bulletin saying the President had been seriously, perhaps fatally, injured by an assassin's bullets while driving through the streets of Dallas.

Litters [stretchers] bearing the President and the governor then rolled by as my back was turned.

I knew they had passed, however, from the horrified expression that suddenly spread over the face of the clerk.

I watched a swift and confused panorama sweep before me.

Kilduff raced up and down the hall. Police captains barked at each other. Two priests hurried in behind a Secret Service agent. A police lieutenant ran down the hall with a large carton of blood for transfusions. A doctor came in and said he was responding to a call for "all neurosurgeons."

Last Sacrament

The priests came out and said the President had received the last sacrament of the Roman Catholic Church. They said he was still alive, but not conscious. Members of the Kennedy staff began arriving. They had been behind us in the motorcade, but hopelessly bogged for a time in confused traffic.

Then Kilduff and Wayne Hawks of the White House staff ran by me, shouting that Kilduff would make a statement shortly at the far end of the hospital.

> Fighting to keep his emotions under control, Kilduff [the White House press secretary] said, 'President John Fitzgerald Kennedy died at approximately one o'clock.'

We reached the door of the conference room and there were loud cries of "Quiet!" Fighting to keep his emotions under control, Kilduff said, "President John Fitzgerald Kennedy died at approximately one o'clock."

Pool for Plane

After calling my office I ran back through the hospital to the conference room where a White House aide grabbed me and said Kilduff wanted a pool of three newsmen immediately to fly back to Washington.

I ran down the stairs and into the driveway, only to discover Kilduff had just pulled out in our telephone car.

Charles Roberts of *Newsweek* magazine, Sid Davis of Westinghouse Broadcasting and I got a police officer to take us to the airport in his squad car.

As we piled out of the car about 200 yards from the Presidential aircraft, Kilduff spotted us and said the plane could take two pool men to Washington; that Mr. Johnson was about to take the oath of office aboard the plane and would take off immediately thereafter.

All Circuits Busy

I saw a bank of telephone booths beside the runway and asked if I had time to call in the news. "For God's sake, hurry," he said.

All circuits were busy to the Dallas office and even Washington. I finally called the New York bureau of UPI and told them about the impending inauguration of a new President aboard the airplane.

A Time of Fear

In the years since President Kennedy was shot there has been constant speculation that it was the result of a conspiracy, and many different theories have been offered as to who the conspirators were. But in the hours immediately following the assassination, the public and the government alike feared that the Soviet Union was responsible and that it might have been intended to cause a disruption in United States leadership immediately prior to an attack. This was why Lyndon Johnson was sworn in as president before his plane left the ground in Dallas—to make sure that the world knew that the U.S. chain of command was not broken.

In a 2004 interview with ABC News, journalist Evan Thomas described the general feeling:

> This is the height of the Cold War. And the idea [of] a sneak attack from the Russians was very much on people's minds. So naturally the fear is that this was the first step in a general attack by the Soviet Union. Not just ordinary people, but at the top of govern-

Aboard Air Force One, on which I had made so many trips as a press association reporter covering President Kennedy, all of the shades of the larger main cabin were drawn and the interior was hot and dimly lighted. The plane sat on the ground throughout the Ceremony. Kilduff propelled us to the President's suite two-thirds of the way back in the plane. The room normally could accommodate eight to 10 people seated.

Stood in Center

I wedged inside the door and counted 27 people in this compartment. Mr. Johnson stood in the center with his wife, Lady Bird. U.S. District Judge Sarah T. Hughes, 67, a kindly-faced woman, stood with a small black Bible in her hands, waiting to give the oath.

The compartment became hotter and hotter. Mr. Johnson was worried that some of the Kennedy staff

ment, that's the first thing that they're wondering about. Is this an attack to decapitate our leader, so they can come in and nuke us? We had scared the hell out of each other in the Cuban Missile Crisis the year before. We have to remember that memory of that near miss was still fresh in people's minds.

And so, Thomas said:

The most important thing the United States government wanted to do was reassure the public that there was not some plot, not some Russian attack, not some Cuban attack. It was to calm and soothe fears, real fears, that this was somehow some nefarious Communist plot. And that the number one goal throughout the upper levels of the government was to calm that fear, and bring a sense of reassurance that this really was the work of a lone gunman.

might not be able to get inside. He urged people to press forward, but a Signal Corps photographer, Capt. Cecil Stoughton, standing in the corner on a chair, said if Mr. Johnson moved any closer, it would be virtually impossible to make a truly historic photograph.

It developed that Mr. Johnson had been waiting for Mrs. Kennedy, who was composing herself in a small bedroom in the rear of the plane. She appeared alone, dressed in the same pink wool suit she had worn in the morning when she appeared so happy shaking hands with airport crowds at the side of her husband.

She was white-faced but dry-eyed. Friendly hands stretched toward her as she stumbled slightly. Mr. Johnson took both of her hands in his and motioned her to his left side. Lady Bird stood on his right, a fixed half-smile showing the tension.

Mr. Johnson nodded to Judge Hughes, an old friend of his family and a Kennedy appointee.

"Hold up your right hand and repeat after me," the woman jurist said to Mr. Johnson.

Outside, a jet could be heard droning into a landing.

Judge Hughes held out the Bible and Mr. Johnson covered it with his large left hand. His right arm went slowly into the air and the jurist began to intone the constitutional oath, "I do solemnly swear I will faithfully execute the office of President of the United States. . . . "

Kissed Her Cheek

The brief ceremony ended when Mr. Johnson, in a deep, firm voice, repeated after the judge, ". . . and so help me God."

Mr. Johnson turned first to his wife, hugged her about the shoulders and kissed her on the cheek. Then he turned to President Kennedy's widow, put his left arm around her and kissed her cheek.

As others in the group—some Texas Democratic House members, members of the Johnson and Kennedy staffs—moved toward the new President, he seemed to back away from any expression of felicitation.

The two-minute ceremony concluded at 3:38 P.M. EST and seconds later President Johnson said firmly, "Now, let's get airborne."

Room Only for Two

Col. James Swindal, pilot of the plane, a big gleaming silver and blue fan-jet, cut on the starboard engines immediately. Several persons, including Sid Davis of Westinghouse, left the plane at that time. The White House had room for only two pool reporters on the return flight and these posts were filled by Roberts and me, although at the moment we could find no empty seats.

At 3:47 P.M. EST, the wheels of Air Force One cleared the runway. Swindal roared the big ship up to an unusually high cruising altitude of 41,000 feet, where at 625 miles an hour, ground speed, the jet hurtled toward Andrews Air Force Base outside Washington.

When the President's plane reached operating altitude, Mrs. Kennedy left her bedchamber and walked to the rear compartment of the plane. This was the so-called family living room, a private area where she and Mr. Kennedy, family and friends had spent many happy airborne hours chatting and dining together.

Casket in Room

Mr. Kennedy's casket had been placed in this compartment, carried aboard by a group of Secret Service agents.

> 'We feel like the heart has been cut out of us,' Mrs. Johnson said.

Mrs. Kennedy went into the rear lounge and took a chair beside the coffin. There she remained throughout the flight. Her vigil was shared at times by four staff members close to the slain Chief Executive—David Powers, his buddy and personal assistant; Kenneth P. O'Donnell, appointments secretary and key political adviser; Lawrence O'Brien, chief Kennedy liaison man with Congress; and Brig. Gen. Godfrey McHugh, Mr. Kennedy's Air Force aide.

Mr. Kennedy's military aide, Maj. Gen. Chester V. Clifton, was busy most of the trip in the forward areas of the plane, sending messages and making arrangements for arrival ceremonies and movement of the body to Bethesda Naval Hospital.

Typewriter Lost

As the flight progressed, Mr. Johnson walked back into the main compartment. My portable typewriter was lost somewhere around the hospital and I was writing on an oversized electric typewriter which Mr. Kennedy's personal secretary, Mrs. Evelyn Lincoln, had used to type his speech texts.

Mr. Johnson came up to the table where Roberts and I were trying to record the history we had just witnessed.

"I'm going to make a short statement in a few minutes and give you copies of it," he said. "Then when I get on the ground, I'll do it over again."

Brief and Moving

It was the first public utterance of the new Chief Executive, brief and moving:

"This is a sad time for all people. We have suffered a loss that cannot be weighed. For me it is a deep personal tragedy. I know the world shares the sorrow that Mrs. Kennedy and her family bear. I will do my best. That is all I can do. I ask for your help—and God's."

When the plane was about 45 minutes from Washington, the new President got on a special radio-telephone and placed a call to Mrs. Rose Kennedy, the late President's mother.

"I wish to God there was something I could do," he told her. "I just wanted you to know that."

Then Mrs. Johnson wanted to talk to the elder Mrs. Kennedy.

"We feel like the heart has been cut out of us," Mrs. Johnson said. She broke down for a moment and began to sob. Recovering in a few seconds, she added, "Our love and our prayers are with you."

Thirty minutes out of Washington, President Johnson put in a call for Nellie Connally, wife of the seriously wounded Texas governor.

The new President said to the governor's wife:

"We are praying for you, darling, and I know that everything is going to be all right, isn't it? Give him a hug and a kiss for me."

It was dark when Air Force One began to skim over the lights of the Washington area, lining up for a landing at Andrews Air Force Base. The plane touched down at 5:59 P.M. EST.

Stood and Watched

I thanked the stewards for rigging up the typewriter for me, pulled on my raincoat and started down the forward ramp. Roberts and I stood under a wing and watched the casket being lowered from the rear of the plane and borne by a complement of armed forces body bearers into a waiting hearse. We watched Mrs. Kennedy and the President's brother, Atty. Gen. Robert F. Kennedy, climb into the hearse beside the coffin.

> It seemed incredible that only six hours before, John Fitzgerald Kennedy had been a vibrant, smiling, waving and active man.

The new President repeated his first public statement for broadcast and newsreel microphones, shook hands with some of the government and diplomatic leaders who turned out to meet the plane, and headed for his helicopter.

Tragedy Summed Up

Roberts and I were given seats on another copter bound for the White House lawn. In the compartment next to ours in one of the large chairs beside a window sat Theodore C. Sorensen, one of Mr. Kennedy's closest associates with the title of special counsel to the President. He had not gone to Texas with his chief but had come to the air base for his return.

Sorensen sat wilted in the large chair, crying softly. The dignity of his deep grief seemed to sum up all of the tragedy and sadness of the previous six hours.

As our helicopter circled in the balmy darkness for a landing on the White House south lawn, it seemed incredible that only six hours before, John Fitzgerald Kennedy had been a vibrant, smiling, waving and active man.

The Grief and Outrage of the American People

Walter Logan

The following news story by a UPI (United Press International) reporter appeared in U.S. newspapers the day after President Kennedy's assassination. It describes the stunned disbelief of the American people, followed first by anger at the assassin, then by grief, tears, and often prayer. All normal activity came to a halt and scheduled events were cancelled. It was lunch hour in most of the nation when the news came; schools and businesses closed early. Flags were lowered to half-staff, and the Olympic torch in the Los Angeles Memorial Coliseum was lighted in Kennedy's honor. Walter Logan was a reporter, and later an editor, for UPI.

SOURCE. Walter Logan, *UPI's 20th Century Top Stories*. Washington, DC: United Press International, 1963.

Grief rolled across the nation like a gigantic shock wave.

First there was stunned disbelief, then hatred and anger at the sniper who shot and killed President Kennedy. And then anguish and tears and prayer.

Not since the assassination of Abraham Lincoln has such spontaneous grief and outrage gripped a nation. Women wept in the streets and men cursed in helpless anger.

> Business came to a standstill as people clustered around radio sets to hear again and again what they could not believe at first.

Business came to a standstill as people clustered around radio sets to hear again and again what they could not believe at first. Still they asked, "Is it true? Is it true?"

The tolling of church bells confirmed their fears.

It was the lunch hour in most of the nation and diners too shattered to eat left their half-finished meals. Shoppers in department stores wandered about misty-eyed and many stores closed.

In New York Mrs. Mary McGrath, an elderly cleaning woman, stopped passersby outside St. Agnes Church and told them, "Jesus, Mary, Mother of God, President Kennedy was shot." When informed he was dead she fell to her knees and wept.

It was a grief stricken city and thousands flocked to St. Patrick's Cathedral as its bells tolled for the president. Stenographers hurriedly tying kerchiefs on their heads sobbed as they ran to the cathedral. The prayerful lighted candles and a bishop recited the rosary, the common denominator used by truck drivers and popes, longshoremen and diplomats.

It was the same throughout the nation. Tears, shock, disbelief.

In Santa Fe, N.M., workmen making repairs in St. Francis Cathedral left their scaffold and knelt before the altar to pray when they heard the news.

> Cars stopped on highways because people could not listen to the news and drive at the same time.

Theaters, movie houses, schools, business houses closed in almost every city. The Metropolitan Opera cancelled a performance of *Gotterdammerung, the Twilight of the Gods*.

Cars stopped on highways because people could not listen to the news and drive at the same time.

Most state governors ordered a 30-day period of mourning and Gov. Nelson Rockefeller of New York ordered a 17-gun salute fired in Albany from 8 A.M. until sundown, a shot every half hour. Albany Mayor Erastus Corning left his office near collapse, tears running down his face.

More than half of the nation's college football games and the entire weekend slate of the American Football League were cancelled—such classics as Yale-Harvard, Duke-North Carolina.

North Carolina State's chancellor refused to cancel the Friday night game between N.C. State and Wake Forest and said Kennedy would have wanted it to go on. State won 42–0.

In Columbia, S.C., a radio station (WCOS) was flooded with calls demanding cancellation of the 61st annual Clemson-South Carolina game. "What have we to cheer about?" a South Carolina cheerleader asked.

In Philadelphia an audience of 2,000 was listening to the Philadelphia Orchestra in the Academy of Music when someone offstage beckoned to conductor Eugene Ormandy.

The maestro left and Henry Peltier, the orchestra manager, came on stage to announce that Kennedy had been assassinated. Cries of anguish rose from the audience and it filed silently out.

In Minneapolis T. Eugene Thompson was on trial for his life for the murder-for-hire death of his wife. The trial was recessed and a woman spectator fell to her knees in tears. She put her hand over her eyes but the tears pushed through and rolled down her wrists.

It was raining in Nashville, Tenn., where crowds huddled near radio and television sets for the latest word. The corridors of the state capitol were abandoned. Outside on the steps 200 Negroes stood silently for a minute of silent prayer and sang the national anthem in the rain.

In California, in Ohio, in Maine, there were cries of "Oh, my God, is he dead? Is he dead?" and angry comments by one man who said, "You don't want to hear what I have to say—I'd like to run wild down there (Texas) with a gun. All they've done is to make him another Lincoln." . . .

The nation's leaders expressed their grief in sorrowful statements. Harry S. Truman called Kennedy's death "a tragedy." Dwight D. Eisenhower, his eyes red, called it a "despicable act." Herbert Hoover said he was "shocked and grieved." . . .

In Salt Lake City, President David O. McKay of the Church of Jesus Christ of Latter Day Saints said "our hearts are filled with sorrow." A group of teen-agers listening to a transistor radio in downtown Salt Lake wept as they listened. . . .

In San Francisco a downtown steak house turned off its piped-in music and hooked up a radio broadcast to the amplifying system. Patrons sat motionless, stunned, letting the food grow cold.

In Reno, Nev., shows were closed but the casinos continued to run full blast. A sobbing woman in Las Vegas telephoned the UPI [United Press International] in New York to express her shock that the gambling never stopped—"it was as if someone had merely fired a shot into the air, as if a toy balloon might have popped." . . .

In Chicago Roosevelt University students thronged around a TV set in the student lounge discussing the possible motives for the shooting. When the death bulletin came, only sobs broke the silence of the group.

Because of This
NATIONAL DISGRACE
AND IN RESPECT TO OUR GREAT PRESIDENT
John F. Kennedy
THIS STORE WILL BE... CLOSED
UNTIL MONDAY NOVEMBER 25th 1963
DAILY NEWS
NEW YORK'S PICTURE NEWSPAPER
5¢
FINAL
PRESIDENT KILLED
Gov. Connally Shot; Suspect Seized; Johnson Is Sworn In

And a Chicago janitor added, "When they get the man who did this, I hope they don't execute him. I'd rather they put him in prison and let the convicts have him. They'd know what to do."

In Washington, crowds gathered across from the Executive Mansion and stared across the street at the flag at half staff, speaking only occasionally and then in hushed tones. The crowd was shocked, unbelieving and angry. In the background a church bell tolled every 20 seconds.

In Dallas there was shock and anger and consternation and shame that the assassination would take place there. All business closed immediately and a big parade that was to have started the Christmas shopping season today was cancelled. . . .

In Kansas City, Mo., 7th graders in Milburn Junior High sat in stunned silence, their minds miles away. At Hunter College in New York City girls became hysterical and ran screaming through the hallways shouting "It's true, it's true."

In a Kansas City tavern a man walked in and complained about the falling stock market. The bartender said he felt like belting the guy but just told him to "get the hell out."

Alabama Gov. George Wallace, who had clashed with Kennedy over the civil rights issue, ordered the state into a thirty-day period of mourning. . . . Arkansas Gov. Orval Faubus, who also clashed with Kennedy over civil rights, said, "This is a tragedy of the greatest magnitude. It is shocking beyond belief and seems incomprehensible. The president was a great American, the chosen leader of his people."

In Meridian, Miss., James Meredith, the Negro whose enrollment at the University of Miss. touched off rioting, said Kennedy "was for the Negro as being full American citizens." He said the death was a "shocking thing."

In Atlanta, Ga., Negro leaders halted their civil rights demonstrations and called for a period of mourning.

Photo on previous page: President Kennedy's assassination left U.S. citizens in grief, shock, and disbelief. (© **Bettmann/ Corbis.**)

JOHN F. KENNEDY'S JOB APPROVAL RATINGS TREND

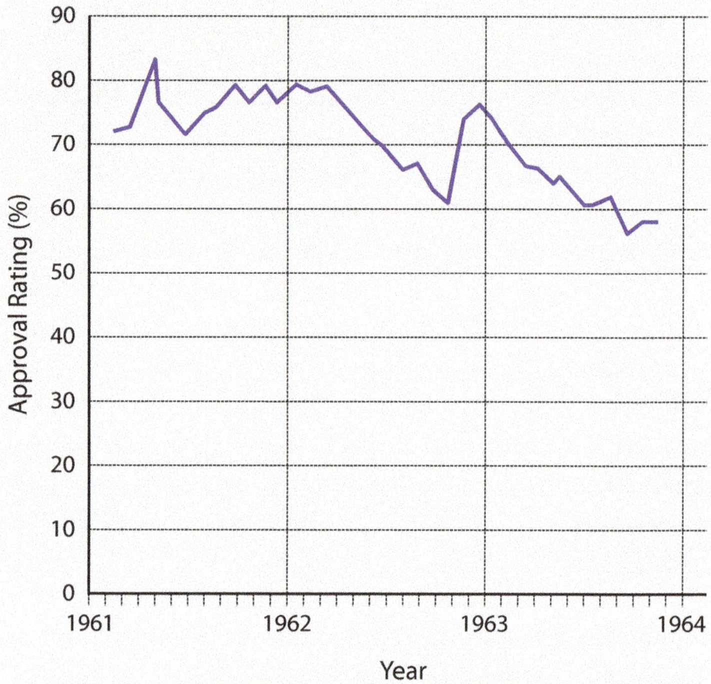

Taken from: Gallup, Inc., "Presidential Approval Ratings—Gallup Historical Statistics and Trends." www.gallup.com.

They called on Negro ministers to lead their congregations in a period of mourning "due to the loss of this great American."

Four hundred University of North Carolina students gathered near the spot where Kennedy delivered a talk in 1961 and bowed their heads below a flag at half staff while an Air Force Band bugler blew "Taps."

In South Bend, Ind., hundreds of students and faculty streamed into the University of Notre Dame chapel, some saying their prayers aloud, to offer what may have been the first high mass for the late president.

At Yale University Prof. Frederick C. Barghoorn, whose release from a Moscow prison was attributed in large part to Kennedy's intercession, called the assassination a "catastrophic, staggering event."

In Charleston, W. Va., where Kennedy participated in centennial Statehood Day ceremonies last June [1963], there was more shock and grief. The statehouse was closed and many schools sent their pupils home.

Southern Californians were devastated by the news and most reacted with stunned silence. Silent crowds stood outside shops listening to news broadcasts. People wept openly when realization finally came. Streets were jammed, particularly around newspaper buildings as people rushed to buy papers flesh off the press.

The Pacific Coast Stock Exchange suspended trading and the Olympic torch in the famed Los Angeles Memorial Coliseum was lighted in Kennedy's honor.

The 11th Naval District in San Diego ordered all ships at sea and in port to lower their flags to half mast.

Mexico closed off the border from the Pacific Coast to the Gulf of Mexico to prevent any assassin from fleeing south. The action brought huge traffic jams—both pedestrian and car—and those who travel across the border regularly were stranded.

In McAllen, Tex., an elderly man identified as A.W. Plath was so shocked he died of an apparent heart attack. Authorities said he heard the news over a television station, murmured "Oh, my God" and died. . . .

Spokesmen for Roman Catholic, Jewish, and Protestant clergy and communicants issued a joint statement asking prayers for Kennedy and for President Johnson.

Tributes to President Kennedy from World Leaders

London *Times*

The following news report appeared in the venerable British newspaper, the *Times*, the day after President Kennedy was assassinated. It contains statements made by many world leaders expressing their shock and sympathy, as well as their admiration for Kennedy. Many of the leaders also sent personal condolences to Mrs. Kennedy.

The death of President Kennedy has caused widespread shock and consternation throughout the world. Tributes to him were pouring in last night.

BONN—Professor [Ludwig] Erhard, the West German Chancellor, who flew back to Bonn by special aircraft from Paris spoke of his "deep shock" at the news. President Kennedy, he said, had been a friend and true ally of the German people who in many difficult hours had much to thank for his steadfastness and coolness.

Professor Erhard's visit to Washington next week has been cancelled. It is likely that [West German] President [Karl Heinrich] Lübke and the Chancellor will attend the funeral ceremonies. [The first Chancellor of West Germany] Dr. [Konrad Hermann] Adenauer may also be present at his own initiative.

OTTAWA—Mr. [Lester B.] Pearson, the Canadian Prime Minister, told the House of Commons: "The world can ill afford at this time to lose a man of his courage. It is a tragedy not only for his family but for all of us". The House adjourned until Monday as a mark of respect.

SYDNEY—"This is a national tragedy for the United States and, for the rest of us, a world calamity", said Sir Robert Menzies, the [Australian] Prime Minister. "The loss of a man with such a capacity for leadership will, for a time, at least, increase dangers of world tension".

"Our Friend"

TEL AVIV—Mr. Lei Eshkol, the Prime Minister of Israel, said Mr. Kennedy had been "a great and dynamic President, and a courageous leader of the free world".

WELLINGTON—The New Zealand Prime Minister, Mr. Keith Holyoake, said: "My mind refuses to accept his death." The Labour Opposition leader, Mr. Arnold Nordmeyer—"We New Zealanders looked on him as a friend who stood for those ideals dear to our hearts".

> 'This is a national tragedy for the United States and, for the rest of us, a world calamity', said . . . the [Australian] prime minister.

KARACHI—"I cannot find words strong enough to condemn such a dastardly act", said President Ayub [Khan]. He extended Pakistan's condo-

Camelot: One Brief Shining Moment

A week after President Kennedy's assassination, the Pulitzer Prize-winning author Theodore H. White interviewed his widow and wrote an article for *Life* magazine that was widely read. "All I keep thinking of is this line from a musical comedy," Jacqueline Kennedy told him. "At night, before we'd go to sleep, Jack liked to play some records. . . . The lines he loved to hear were: *Don't let it be forgot, that once there was a spot, for one brief shining moment that was known as Camelot.*" Those words are from the musical *Camelot*, a story about the legendary King Arthur and the knights of the Round Table. "Jack had this hero idea of history, the idealistic view," Mrs. Kennedy said. White concluded his article, which was titled "For President Kennedy, An Epilogue," by stating, "For one brief shining moment there was Camelot."

The day that issue of *Life* came out, *Camelot* was playing at the Chicago Opera House. Writer Mark Steyn quoted Alan Jay Lerner—"the show's author and a friend of Jack Kennedy's since

lences to Mrs. Kennedy and the "United States Government and people".

BELGRADE—[Yugoslav] President [Josip Broz] Tito telephoned the American Chargé d'Affaires to express "deep sympathy".

THE HAGUE—Dr. [Victor] Marijnen, the Dutch Prime Minister, said the death of Mr. Kennedy was "an international disaster".

TEHERAN—The Shah of Iran decreed national mourning.

LISBON—Dr. Franco Nogueira, the Portuguese Foreign Minister, said that Portugal would go into three days' mourning. Both Dr. [Antonío de Oliveira] Salazar, the Prime Minister, and President Americo Thomaz have sent telegrams of condolence to President Lyndon Johnson.

MADRID—[Spanish] General [Francisco] Franco said he was "profoundly shocked by the news" of the as-their schooldays at Choate"—in the August 13, 2007, issue of *Maclean's* recalling that day:

> When it came to those lines, . . . there was a sudden wail from the audience. . . . The play stopped, and for almost five minutes everyone in the theatre—on the stage, in the wings, in the pit and in the audience—wept without restraint. *Camelot* had suddenly become the symbol of those one thousand days when people the world over saw a bright new light of hope shining from the White House.

The thousand days of Kennedy's presidency were soon referred to as Camelot by the media, and the metaphor was emphasized in a biography of Kennedy by William Manchester. Ever since, it has been used to express the hope his leadership brought to the nation and his admirers' regret that it had come to an end so soon.

sassination. President Kennedy had led "the American nation in difficult moments and was a great statesmanlike figure in the Christian west".

HELSINKI—Radio stations throughout Finland cancelled their scheduled programmes after news of the President's death and broadcast mourning music for the rest of the night.

BRUSSELS—[Belgian] King Baudouin in a message to President Johnson said: "We shall preserve the great memory of him who dedicated all his forces to the good of his fatherland, peace and freedom in the world".

NORTHERN IRELAND—Captain Terence O'Neill, Prime Minister of Northern Ireland, who is in London, sent condolences to Mr. Robert Kennedy, the late President's brother.

LONDON—Sir Harold Caccia, Permanent Under-Secretary at the Foreign Office and first British Ambas-

After the assassination, Willy Brandt, who ran the city of West Berlin, called Kennedy "the first citizen of the free world." **(Walter Sanders/Time Life Pictures/Getty Images.)**

sador to be accredited to President Kennedy, said he would be remembered in Britain "for his concern for peace and his judgment, firmness, and understanding in pursuing the ideals which inspire free men".

> Moscow radio broke into its programme to [announce]: 'Comrades, radio listeners, we have interrupted our broadcast because of the sorrowful report which has just been received from New York'.

BERLIN—Herr [Willy] Brandt, the chief burgomaster, said in a broadcast: "With the first citizen of the free world, Berlin lost its best friend". He asked the people of Berlin to honour Mr. Kennedy by placing candles in the windows tonight.

MOSCOW—Moscow radio broke into its programme to make the following announcement: "Comrades, radio listeners, we have interrupted our broadcast because of the sorrowful report which has just been received from New York". It then gave the news of the shooting of President Kennedy. It did not resume its normal programme later but began broadcasting solemn organ music.

OSLO—Mr. [Einar] Gerhardsen, the Norwegian Prime Minister, expressed his and the nation's sympathy for Mrs. Kennedy, her children, and the American nation.

ATHENS—King Paul, in a message to Mr. Lyndon Johnson, conveyed the sincere sympathy of the Greek nation and himself. The King and Queen sent their personal condolences to Mrs. Kennedy. Mr. [George] Papandreou, the Prime Minister, said he was "profoundly shocked" by the news.

ANKARA—President [Cemal] Gursel described President Kennedy in a broadcast as "a pioneer in the great struggles of humanity, a determined fighter for world peace, and a firm friend of the Turkish nation".

SALISBURY—Sir Roy Welensky, Prime Minister of the Rhodesian Federation, said he was "stunned", adding "my immediate reaction is intense sympathy for Mrs. Kennedy and the family".

COPENHAGEN—Mr. [Jens Otto] Krag, the Danish Prime Minister, spoke of "an untiring advocate of peace and freedom" and said Mr. Kennedy's death "will leave a black spot on our time".

SANTIAGO—[Chilean] President [Jorge] Alessandri expressed his "profound consternation" at the news of President Kennedy's assassination.

CAIRO—[Egyptian] President [Gamal Abdel] Nasser described Mr. Kennedy as "struggling for his people and humanity".

DELHI—[Indian] President [Sarvepalli] Radhakrishnan said Mr. Kennedy was "a man of great courage and conscience".

NEW YORK—Former President [Dwight] Eisenhower described the assassination as a "despicable act". He said he was sure the nation "will join as one man in expressing not only grief and indignation at this act, but will also stand faithful to the Government".

Governor [Nelson] Rockefeller, of New York, a candidate for the Republican Presidential nomination in 1965, said in a statement: "May God grant strength and guidance to Lyndon Johnson as he assumes his great responsibilities under these tragic circumstances".

The Reaction of the Russian People to Kennedy's Death

Robert Brigham

The following article was written in Moscow and published two weeks after Kennedy's assassination in the popular American magazine *Life*. It describes the grief felt by ordinary Russian people—a reaction that surprised Americans because the two countries were then at odds. At that time the Soviet Union usually censored the news, and its people had been told that President Kennedy was a good man whose desire for peace was opposed by radicals in the Senate and the Pentagon. As a result, in addition to mourning for him, Russians feared that Kennedy's opponents had decided to eliminate him and that the danger of war had therefore increased. Robert Brigham was a correspondent for *Life* magazine.

SOURCE. Robert Brigham, "Russia: 'No, No, This Cannot Be True'," *Life*, vol. 55, December 6, 1963, pp. 129–130.

Night had fallen in Moscow and a wet snow was coming down hard. Most residents of the city were at home, and those who owned television sets were watching a rather dull evening of programs.

The ten o'clock news came on and the newscaster routinely began to tick off the items. Suddenly a technician raced into camera view and dropped a paper on the newscaster's desk—the first time anybody can remember such a thing happening on Moscow television. The announcer started, then read the bare-bones bulletin of the shooting of the President of the United States. Then came the news of his death. The announcer read it to himself, then looked up into the camera in disbelief, repeating the words as though talking to himself.

A few moments later, in the popular cafe of the Hotel Ukraine, the word was suddenly passed to waiters, cooks and busboys to gather in the central kitchen. The manager told them the news. A moment of silence, then the scattered cries of protest: "No! The comrade manager is wrong. No, no! This cannot be true!"

> "Only in the morning came the full realization that it had not all been a dream, a realization heightened by the astounding reaction of the Russians."

The American residents of Moscow consist almost solely of embassy personnel and journalists and, by decree, they live in an island apart, in the apartment houses reserved for foreigners. The first word of the shooting of the President filtered into many of these homes through the static that punctuates the overseas short-wave broadcasts from the Voice of America. Friends called friends to make sure they had heard, and in every apartment, the phone rang ten, a dozen, fifteen times. Guests at a half-dozen dinner parties left their dessert and coffee to search desperately across the dial for a signal strong enough to bridge the miles. Then the men left for their offices.

Only in the morning came the full realization that it had not all been a dream, a realization heightened by the astounding reaction of the Russians.

Admiration for Kennedy

There was, for example, the chauffeur who called to pick up one American who had ordered a car. Knowing almost no English, the chauffeur searched for the words as he stood stiffly at attention, hat held before him in both hands. He finally said, "President Kennedy great man."

A young electronics engineer, whose first name is Valery, had heard the first bulletins on the ten o'clock news telecast. After listening to the meager details he bolted out of his apartment. His neighbors had heard the television announcement, so Valery borrowed five rubles and ran through the falling snow to find a taxi and go half way across the city to some other friends who had no television set or telephone. They spent the rest of the night talking about the assassination.

> 'We worry that there are no other men strong enough really to keep up the search for a way for all of us to live in peace.'

Next day they met again at lunch in the center of the city to talk some more. I stopped and spoke to Valery. "We are in deep sorrow," he said. "We sympathize, but we feel that this loss is almost as great, as tragic, to us as it is to you. This was the first man—the only man—to try and find a path on which we both could meet. We worry that there are no other men strong enough really to keep up the search for a way for all of us to live in peace."

And there was Vladimir, a truck driver, waiting at the Moscow Central Post Office to put through a call to his family out in the country. "This tragedy strikes me very close to my heart," he told me. "He was a man of my generation. We were born in the same year. We fought in the same war. He knew what war was like and so do I. This

ERICA
DANGER
KEEP AWAY

being in a war then trying to rebuild the country afterward and build a life—I think it makes a man a realist, sensible. I think most of the men of our age who fought together are realists, and sensible."

Fears for the Future

On the morning after the assassination, one American housewife opened her apartment door to let in the newly employed Russian cleaning woman. The tears were streaming down the Russian woman's face and her eyes were red. She tried to comfort the American but with each word and touch of condolence the tears welled up again. Finally the woman left. But not before she had choked out the question that has become a dirge here, "What will happen to us now?" Then, "Why, oh why?"

> Many Russians reasoned, in despair, that the 'wild men' had simply decided to eliminate President Kennedy and were taking over.

In a cafe three university students shared one copy of *Pravda* over their beer. "Tell us what this means," one asked me. "How could this happen in America, of all countries?"

"It was the work of a madman," I told them, and they accepted the explanation. "But what will this mean for the future?" they asked.

This is the one question that all Russians are asking now as the shock ebbs. The esteem that most Russian people had for John Kennedy, and the fears they now have for the future, are twin byproducts of the way in which they get their news. The Russian press has long taken the position—particularly since the signing of the test-ban treaty—that President Kennedy was a reasonable man seriously dedicated to peace, but was all too often hamstrung by "wild men" in the Senate, the Pentagon, the State Department of the South. Many Russians reasoned, in despair, that the "wild men" had

Photo on previous page: After Kennedy's death, some Russians worried about what kind of president Lyndon Johnson would be. **(John Dominis/ Time Life Pictures/Getty Images.)**

An Eternal Flame

At the conclusion of the service at Arlington National Cemetery that followed John F. Kennedy's funeral, his widow Jacqueline Kennedy—watched by television audiences worldwide—took a candle from a soldier and lighted an eternal flame at his grave. Mrs. Kennedy's desire for this memorial was inspired by the one at the Tomb of the Unknown Soldier at the Arc de Triomphe in Paris, and the military funeral organizers rushed to implement her request. Fed by an underground gas line and automatically reignited whenever extinguished by wind or rain, the flame has been kept burning ever since.

For the first two years after Kennedy's death, soldiers stood vigil at the gravesite. Then a new and more elaborate gravesite was constructed at the same location, necessitated by the large number of visitors and the need for paved paths that would not turn to mud in wet weather. Jacqueline Kennedy, who died in 1994, is now buried next to President Kennedy, as are their infant son Patrick and a stillborn daughter born earlier. The graves of his brothers Robert and Ted are nearby.

In 1964 a postage stamp was issued depicting the flame. On it are words from President Kennedy's inaugural address: "And the glow from that fire can truly light the world."

simply decided to eliminate President Kennedy and were taking over.

Contributing to this feeling is the fact that the Russians know practically nothing about Lyndon Johnson. "Tell us about Johnson," the three students asked worriedly. "Is he a good man, like Kennedy was a good man?" Then one of the students brightened with sudden hope. "You know, we didn't know anything at all about Kennedy when he became President. Only that he was rich. We did not trust him at first. But we came to know him better through his words, his actions. Then we could trust him. Maybe it will be the same with Johnson."

No Censorship

As the hours passed, and then the days, Russia accepted the fact of the President's death. On Sunday night, the eve of the funeral, four million Russian television viewers heard somber music from their sets, and on the screen saw the black-bordered portrait of John F. Kennedy. Then, in a documentary-style presentation, came film clips from the brief Kennedy career in the White House. Most incredible of all was one filmed sequence showing him making a speech translated into Russian, of his opposition to racial discrimination. Until then, Russians had been led to believe that mistreatment of American Negroes, if not actually sanctioned, is opposed hardly at all by the U.S. government.

The following night those millions of viewers went once again to their sets, this time to watch his funeral procession and the array of world leaders entering the Washington cathedral. They were seeing all this relayed from half the world away by the American communications satellite Telstar, at the moment it was happening, with no interposing of censorship.

Now the funeral is over and the making of politics and the staking out of the official line have begun. The Russian press has mounted an attack against the "ultras" whom they accuse of killing both the President and [his assassin] Lee Harvey Oswald. But many Russians are still accosting Americans to ask their question directly: "Why did it have to happen?"

The Reaction of the African People to Kennedy's Death

Philip E. Muehlenbeck

President John F. Kennedy was greatly admired in Africa, and the news of his assassination spread rapidly there. In Nairobi, Kenya, a crowd of six thousand attended a memorial service for him. Throughout Africa not only city dwellers but the people of isolated villages mourned; even much later pictures of Kennedy were still displayed in their huts. Streets and schools, as well as many individuals, were named after him, for it was felt that he was the first American leader who had understood Africa and its problems. Philip E. Muehlenbeck is an adjunct professor of history at George Washington University.

Africans sensed a genuine sincerity in Kennedy's sympathy for their cause. . . . According to [Senegalese president Léopold Sédar] Senghor,

SOURCE. Philip E. Muehlenbeck, "John F. Kennedy's Courting of African Nationalism," *Madison Historical Review*, vol. 2, September 7, 2004, pp. 18–19. Reproduced by permission of the author.

"African chiefs of state had a feeling of great esteem, I can even say, great admiration, for President Kennedy." Julius Nyerere [president of Tanzania], Ahmed Ben Bella [president of Algeria], Kwame Nkrumah [president of Ghana], and others understood that at times global Cold War considerations and the democratic nature of the American political system prevented Kennedy from doing as much for their continent as he would have liked to. Nonetheless, Africans were touched that a Western leader would show concern for their plight, and were overcome with grief after learning of the American President's assassination.

The news of Kennedy's assassination spread rapidly through Africa—from Algiers to Dar es Salaam, Cairo to Accra, and even in the most distant and isolated villages,

The time and attention President Kennedy devoted to Africa and its people led to great sorrow throughout the continent upon news of his death. **(AP Images.)**

Africans mourned. In Nairobi, Kenya, for example, six thousand people packed a cathedral for the American President's memorial service. Kenyan leader Tom Mboya said that the news of Kennedy's death was deeply felt in his country:

> The shock that was registered in this country was particularly noticeable because it was the first time that the death of a foreigner, and a foreign head of state, had registered so sharply. It was as though someone very close at home had died and people reacted spontaneously in practically every little town and village in this country. . . . I saw very clearly that President Kennedy's personality had penetrated deep in the villages quite remote from the normal political atmosphere of the country. . . . [In Africa] President Kennedy offered much excitement and hope in the future. [Africans] saw in him a young man who understood the modern world and the problems of the younger generation. . . . Another thing is that people saw in President Kennedy, in Africa at any rate, a very enlightened approach insofar as the Cold War was concerned. . . . [Kennedy] gave the world that much more hope.

Days after the tragic events that took place in Dallas, the British Ambassador to the Ivory Coast telegraphed London that Kennedy would soon join [murdered Congolese leader] Patrice Lumumba as an African martyr. The American President, he concluded, had "captured the imagination of the Africans both because of his youth and 'dynamism' and because they regarded him as responsible for the policy of standing up to the (racism in the American) South." Her Majesty's representative in Abidjan [former capital of the Ivory Coast] ended his dispatch by predicting that if Lyndon Johnson continued JFK's policies towards Africa, "the President's death may be found to have given quite a boost to the American effort in this part of the world."

Africans Still Remember Kennedy

Sadly, Johnson did not maintain JFK's policy of courting African nationalists. Yet despite the fact that American policy makers have neglected Africa for so long following his death, Africans still fondly remember the legacy of John F. Kennedy. Sargent Shriver [the driving force behind the Peace Corps] wrote how common it was for him to walk into an African village hut, after his brother-in-law's death, and find a picture of President Kennedy—torn from a newspaper and placed beside the family album or mementos. Visiting Ethiopia, Kenya, and Ghana in the late 1980s, [former Peace Corps director] Harris Wofford found "that in the homes of ordinary people no other American president or world leader had joined the faded photographs of John Kennedy."

Streets, schools, and parks all across Africa were renamed in honor of the slain American President, and his likeness soon graced African currency and stamps. Kennedy's Ambassador to Guinea wrote:

> Streets, schools, and parks all across Africa were renamed in honor of the slain American President, and his likeness soon graced African currency and stamps.

> The President, as I say, was very good at personal diplomacy, and I'm sure that had he had the chance, eventually, to go to Africa, he could have accomplished a great deal. I've found out, after returning to Africa since his death, that the Kennedy legend is very great, and a lot of the good will for our policies is still due to what he said and did in those two-and-a-half years. . . . For example, there are many people in Kenya named after him. Even though he was never in Kenya, many people felt that he was the first American leader who ever really understood Africa.

CHAPTER 2

Controversies Surrounding the Assassination of John F. Kennedy

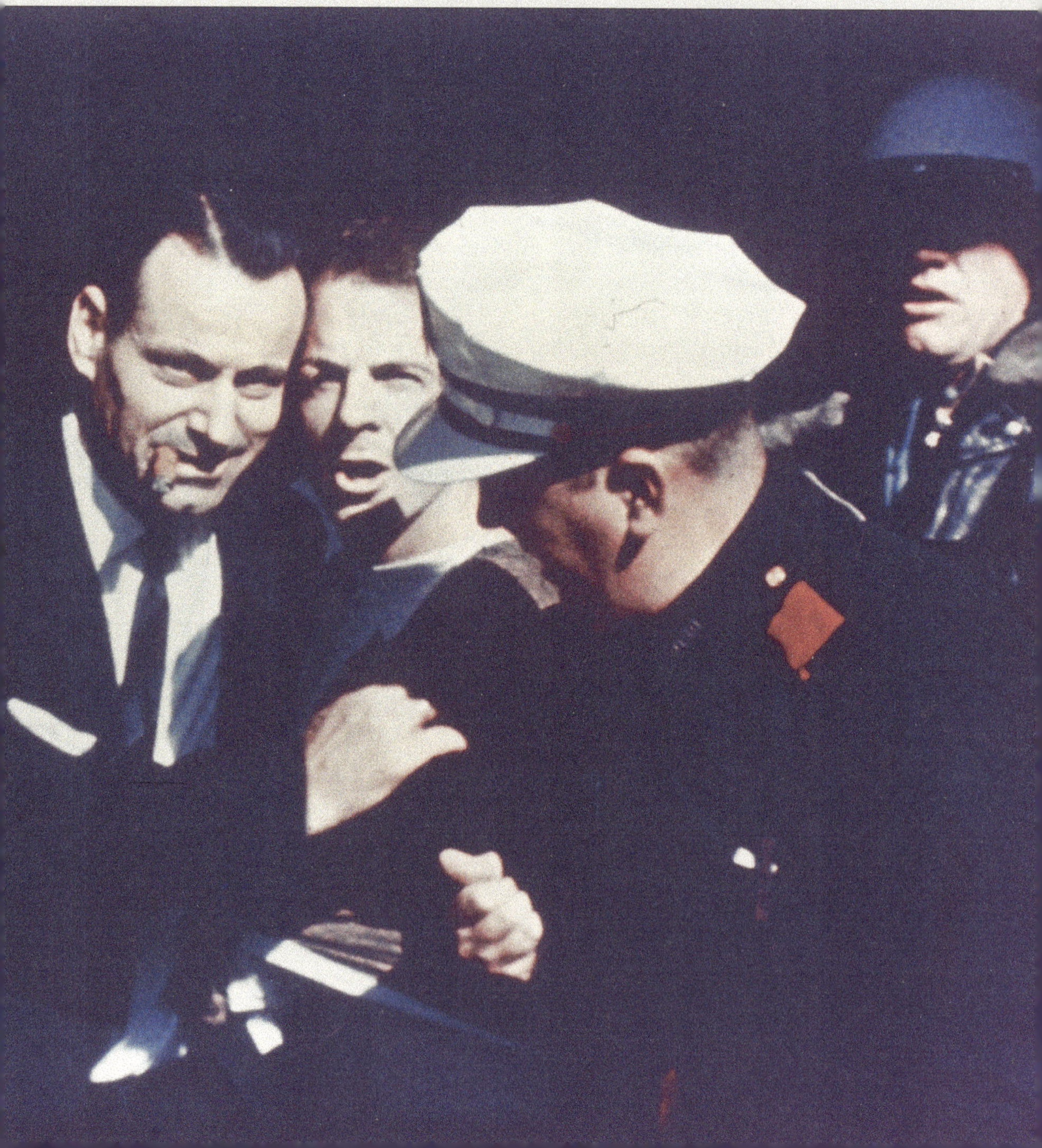

VIEWPOINT 1

Many Nations Thought the Assassination Was the Result of a Right-Wing Conspiracy

Ian Griggs

Ian Griggs visited the United Kingdom's national repository of official records to see what information the British Foreign Office gathered at the time of John F. Kennedy's assassination. The following is an excerpt of his report on what he found. There were documents showing the reactions of the people of many nations, all of whom were concerned about what the loss of President Kennedy would mean to their own future. Few countries accepted the idea that there had been only one deranged assassin. The Soviet Union tried particularly hard to convince the world that it was the work of a right-wing conspiracy. Ian Griggs, a retired British police detective, is editor of the *Dealey Plaza Echo*, the journal of a British research group devoted to the study of the death of JFK.

Photo on previous page: Lee Harvey Oswald, shown (second from left) in police custody in Dallas on November 23, 1963, was charged with President Kennedy's assassination but was murdered himself just a day later. **(Fotoresearch/Getty Images.)**

SOURCE. Ian Griggs, "World Reaction to the Kennedy Assassination," *Assassination Research*, vol. 1, 2002. Copyright © 2002 Ian Griggs. Reproduced by permission.

In the United Kingdom, the Public Record Office (PRO) is the equivalent of the United States National Archives. It is the national repository for all UK governmental and other official records which are to be permanently preserved. . . . Its main building, and by far the largest, is situated at Kew, on the western outskirts of London. It is here that the British Foreign Office records, which include the Kennedy-related files referred to herein, are stored. Records held are normally available for study by members of the public after 30 years. . . .

The main file I studied consists of three smaller related files linked together under the common title "International Reaction to the Death of President Kennedy, 1963." Within each of them there are individual files dealing with reaction in specific countries. Much of the material within consists of communications and reports sent to Her Majesty's Foreign Office in London from British Embassies and Consulates around the world. Most of these had been sent within a week of the assassination—some within just two or three days. Presumably the Foreign Office had requested this information urgently following the assassination of President Kennedy and the murder of [his assassin] Lee Harvey Oswald.

> Every individual country was obviously concerned about its own future and situation following Kennedy's death and the unexpected emergence of Lyndon Johnson as President.

When you study documents like these in some depth, you inevitably get an overall feeling about the situation. As is to be expected, the main feeling is one of shock. Whether you are reading about the reaction of the public in Russia, the Government in France, or British ex-patriots in Australia, that feeling is the same. These papers do not only deal with those countries, however. Also included—and given equal prominence—are countries from the emerging third world in Africa, Asia, and South America.

Every individual country was obviously concerned about its own future and situation following Kennedy's death and the unexpected emergence of Lyndon Johnson as President. Some countries feared a sudden change in American policy towards them. Would existing trade agreements continue as before? Would U.S. aid be cut off? Would there be a change in attitude towards the Eastern Bloc? What would happen in Vietnam?

I learnt that only two countries in the entire world did not treat Kennedy's death with the reverence and respect it deserved. One was Red China and the other, somewhat surprisingly to me, was Portugal. In Communist China, there was nothing in the way of a public tribute and one major newspaper carried a front-page cartoon showing JFK face down in a pool of blood with the caption "Kennedy Bites the Dust." I subsequently learnt that Portugal's cold attitude was due to something of a breakdown in relations with the United States as the result of serious ongoing trade disputes.

"Only two countries in the entire world did not treat Kennedy's death with the reverence and respect it deserved. One was Red China and the other, somewhat surprisingly . . . , was Portugal."

Some Direct Quotes

Allow me to quote directly from some of these files. I think you will, like me, find several of these remarks somewhat prophetic.

1. This is from a file dealing with reactions to the assassination in Czechoslovakia. President Antonin Novotny sent a message of sympathy to the new President in which he said that Kennedy was the victim of a criminal plot. This comment was made as early as 23rd November.

2. Still in Czechoslovakia, the newspaper *Rude Provo* (24th November), quoting the Czech Press Agency in the United States, refers to contradictory rumours as to the forces behind the assassination. Some rumours indicated that the FBI and the CIA are in back of it.
3. Going forward to 25th November, this is from the British Embassy in Peking (now Beijing), China, to the Foreign Office in London. It is an unattributed direct quote from the Chinese press: "The obvious, in fact the only line to take, I should think, is that the United States ruling classes (reactionary, imperialist, etc.) decided that Kennedy was betraying their interests in some way and had to be liquidated."
4. Here is the first of two very positive statements concerning the death of Lee Harvey Oswald. It comes from the Yugoslav newspaper *Borba* of 25th November: "Oswald's murder took place with police connivance." Well, I personally think that the word "connivance" is a little strong at so early a stage—although subsequent research does suggest that there could be some truth in it.
5. Still with the press, there is a wonderful headline in the German newspaper *Neues Deutschland*, again on 25th November. It appears above one of those infamous photographs of Jack Ruby shooting Oswald and says simply (in German, of course): "Dead men tell no tales." Those five short words are as true today as they were when they were penned by an anonymous German headline writer.
6. Remaining with the Oswald murder, here are the comments of an official at the British Embassy in Tokyo, Japan, in a report to the Foreign Office on 26th November: "The shooting of Oswald, the alleged assassin, aroused unfavourable comment in the Japanese press. The impression has been given in some headlines that the United States is a country

where lynch law prevails and the whole episode has, in the opinion of the Japanese press, tarnished the American image abroad."

7. The British Embassy in Buenos Aires, Argentina, sent a lengthy communique to the Foreign Office on 29th November. It included the following rather odd statement: "The quantity of material published, broadcast and televised was staggering; the American Embassy must be far better equipped with obituary material than we are."

8. Now for a brief visit to Africa. This is from an official communication sent from the British Embassy in Khartoum, Sudan, to the Foreign Office. It is dated 6th December—obviously well after the event and at a time when it was possible to judge the situation more objectively. I find this statement strangely prophetic in view of subsequent views and opinions: "Later speculation on the assassin's motives has laid stress on the influence of Zionism and the extreme right in the United States." Well, I don't know about the Zionist angle, but as far as the right wing goes. . . .

9. The final extract I quote here comes from an internal British Government document prepared by the Foreign Office itself on 23rd December—a month and a day after the assassination. It is unclear whether this was intended to be presented to the Prime Minister, the Foreign Secretary, or whoever. It is taken from a lengthy report in which the world is divided into convenient geographical and political boxes for individual comment. Under the heading Eastern Europe, we read the following: "Most eastern bloc countries stuck to the story that President Kennedy had been

> 'Most eastern bloc countries stuck to the story that President Kennedy had been killed by a right wing racist and denounced the killing of Oswald by Ruby as a fascist plot to cover up the truth.'

killed by a right wing racist and denounced the killing of Oswald by Ruby as a fascist plot to cover up the truth."

What Does It All Mean?

The above represents just a small cross-section of the material contained in this file. I have obviously been somewhat selective in my quotes, but it seems that many of the initial opinions have changed very little over the years. I am intrigued by the regularity with which words like "racist" and "fascist" are used to describe the plot.

Not surprisingly, two particular countries were anxious to allay any suspicions that they had been connected with the assassination in any way. Both the Soviet Union and Cuba strongly denied any involvement. Cuba especially seemed gripped with fear that the blame would be laid at its door. Russia was not quite as paranoid but nevertheless stressed from an early date that it was innocent.

I find it interesting—and perhaps significant—that very few countries seemed to accept that the assassination was the act of one deranged lone-nut. That feeling was strengthened when the same deranged lone-nut was dispatched quickly and efficiently by a second deranged lone-nut called Jack Ruby. . . .

A Second Visit to the PRO

On 30th November 2001, knowing that the eighth and final Kennedy Assassination file had been opened and released for public scrutiny, I returned to the Public Record Office. . . .

Marked CONFIDENTIAL, there are two separate parts to this file. The first bears the title "Soviet Foreign Policy in the Light of President Kennedy's Death" and is a lengthy internal Foreign Office Report dated 27th November 1963. It is a very general and non-committal overview which comes to the conclusion that President

Известия

Неделя 47

Иллюстрированное обозрение

17-23 ноября 1963

ТРАГИЧЕСКАЯ ВЕСТЬ ИЗ ТЕХАСА: ЗЛОДЕЙСКОЕ УБИЙСТВО ПРЕЗИДЕНТА США ДЖОНА КЕННЕДИ

Джон Фитцджеральд КЕННЕДИ

Soviet media swiftly blamed Kennedy's death on various right-wing U.S. groups, while disavowing any responsibility. (AP Images.)

Johnson's assumption of office does not suggest that any sudden change in Soviet policy is planned and that the Soviet leaders will probably adopt a wait-and-see policy. It was stressed that the Soviets remained embarrassed at Oswald's alleged Communist and Cuban connections and that they continued to deny that he was ever a member of the American Communist Party or was connected with any pro-Cuban movement.

Mentioning Kennedy's strong handling of the Berlin situation within six months of taking office, however, it is stated that we cannot exclude the possibility that [Soviet Premier Nikita] Khrushchev will again be tempted to see whether the new President has the strength and determination to withstand a crisis.

Of historical as well as political interest, it is mentioned that Soviet television made use of Telstar (the world's first low-altitude active communications satellite) to transmit pictures directly from Washington. (I am tempted to ask if the shooting of Oswald was also shown live in Moscow, and if so, what reaction it caused.) . . .

Soviet Press Coverage

[Another] file is concerned with daily media coverage of the assassination in the Soviet Union. It explains that the first news of an attempt on Kennedy's life was given in the Moscow Home Service (radio) at 19.28 GMT (1:28 PM CST). It then quotes the principal Soviet newspapers. *Pravda* stressed that Kennedy had insisted that Congress should ratify the Nuclear Test Ban Treaty despite sharp attacks from the American "wild men." On Sunday 24th November, *Nedelya*, the *Izvestiya* weekly supplement, published a large photograph of President Kennedy on its front page under the headline "Tragic News from Texas: Villainous Assassination of President John Kennedy."

Moscow Radio continued major coverage of the assassination as the news came in and a Tass dispatch from Washington blamed the Birchites [John Birch Society, an extreme right-wing organization] and the Ku Klux Klan.

It appears that during the period between the 22nd and the 24th, the Soviet media was at great pains to indicate that the assassination was a carefully planned political plan and that the police authorities . . . were striving to implicate the left-wing forces apparently in an effort to channel the anger and indignation of the American people away from the real culprits. . . .

Not surprisingly, the Soviet media, particularly the press, used Jack Ruby's successful attack upon Oswald to further distance their country from the assassination. A direct connection between the two men was mentioned on the 25th and it was claimed that they had been seen together at Ruby's club the day before the assassination. Once again, there were strenuous denials that Oswald had ever been a member of the Communist Party. . . .

On 27th and 28th November, Soviet communications media were devoting more space to the suspicious circumstances of Oswald's death than to the assassination itself. At the same time, however, President Johnson was being given a generally favourable press.

Pravda (28th) carried several reports from foreign sources to support claims that right-wing extremists were responsible for the murders of both Kennedy and Oswald. These included pieces under headlines such as "Who armed the murderer?" (Rio de Janeiro), "Revealing details" (Rome), "Too many missing pieces" (Paris), and "Were there too many snipers?" (Vienna). There was also a report from Paris that one of Ruby's former dancers had stated that he had been hired to kill Oswald and had been paid for it. . . .

[The last] sub-file contains just one document, this being the CONFIDENTIAL report sent direct to the British Foreign Office by the British Ambassador in Moscow. It is dated 6th December 1963. The title of the report is "Soviet Reactions to the Assassination of President Kennedy" and it opens with the following summary:

> The news of President Kennedy's assassination provoked immediate expressions of genuine regret and sympathy on the part of the Soviet authorities and the Soviet

> people (paragraphs 1–3).
>
> The Soviet Press, radio and television gave the event widespread coverage and soon adopted the line that the assassination was the work of right wing extremists (paragraphs 4–7).
>
> The Soviet Government has good reason to regret President Kennedy's death. We are unlikely to see any change in Soviet policy in the near future as a result of President Kennedy's disappearance from the scene (paragraph 8).

This official report, carefully prepared two weeks after the assassination of President Kennedy, is couched in straightforward, non-sensational terms. As can be seen from the Summary, it indicates that the Soviet media in general had continued to maintain that the assassination was the work of right wing extremists. Whether this was a genuinely held view or just intended to deflect possible blame from the Soviet Union is unclear. It was also repeated that Soviet policy was unlikely to change following President Kennedy's disappearance from the scene. (What a classic euphemism those four words present!)

> In the days and weeks following the assassination, the world was in complete confusion. . . . It quickly became a period of intense insecurity, uncertainty and fear.

Once again, it was pointed out that the Soviet press had continued to intimate that the Dallas Police of whom they had nothing good to say . . . were not merely inefficient but were implicated either in the assassination itself or in attempts to hush it up.

A Period of Uncertainty

The overall impression I gained from my two visits to the PRO, particularly my first, was that in the days and weeks following the assassination, the world was in complete confusion. I can recall my own thoughts at the time. It quickly became a period of intense insecurity, uncertainty and fear. Looking back on it now, I personally feel that we could well have been closer to nuclear war in the two or three weeks after 22nd November 1963 that we had been even at the height of the Cuban Missile Crisis the year before.

Fortunately, the Soviet Union felt it more important to sit back and concentrate on vociferously maintaining its own innocence than to take any more positive action. One can only speculate on the outcome had the Soviets decided that this time of confusion could provide the opportunity to launch a successful physical attack upon the United States and her allies. From the files quoted above, it seems they were far too busy implicating the Dallas Police Department in the Kennedy and Oswald murders than in pressing the red nuclear button.

VIEWPOINT 2

Critics of the Official Explanation of the Assassination Have No Real Evidence

William Rubinstein

The following article explains the work of the Warren Commission, which conducted the official investigation into the Kennedy assassination, and the case against its conclusion. Although no one has ever been able to disprove the report, by the 1980s polls showed that 80 percent of the public did not believe it. The article goes on to present arguments in favor of the Warren Commission Report and to assert that the amateur historians who have contested it have not been searching for facts with an open mind. William Rubinstein is a professor of modern history at the University of Wales, Aberystwyth.

SOURCE. William Rubinstein, "Oswald Shoots JFK but Who Is the Real Target?" *History Today*, vol. 49, October 1999, p. 15.

The assassination of John F. Kennedy in Dallas, Texas, on November 22, 1963, was one of the watershed events of the twentieth century. Everyone who remembers it also knows where they were when they heard the news. If (as is often suggested) it led to America's disastrous involvement in Vietnam, it was also one of the most momentous. Yet it is one of contemporary history's most enduring mysteries. Although the apparent assassin was arrested within ninety minutes of the killing, the assassination has often been termed the greatest unsolved crime in American history. A Presidential commission of inquiry headed by the [United States Supreme Court] Chief Justice Earl Warren concluded in 1964 that Lee Harvey Oswald, the alleged assassin, acted alone, and that Jack Ruby, who killed Oswald two days after the assassination, also acted alone, but many hundreds of books and articles have been written to prove that Kennedy was assassinated as a result of a far-reaching conspiracy. Not one of these critics of the Warren Report is a professional historian, yet their efforts probably constitute the largest body of work by amateur historians on any single subject. Astonishingly, to the best of my knowledge, no academic historian has ever investigated Kennedy's assassination and the theories surrounding it. [This is no longer true.]

"Many hundreds of books and articles have been written to prove that Kennedy was assassinated as a result of a far-reaching conspiracy."

Lee Harvey Oswald

Although Lee Harvey Oswald (1939–63) was only twenty-four at the time of the killing, his life had already been so strange as to seem out of a novel. Oswald's father died young and his itinerant mother had lived in several American cities. As a teenager in New York he encountered left-wing political propaganda and became an

Although the Warren Commission put huge effort into probing Kennedy's murder, others have devoted vast effort into assailing the commission's findings. **(AP Images.)**

avowed Marxist. Oswald was a keen reader, a loner, and a classic autodidact. He saw, however, no contradiction in joining the US Marines at only sixteen while at the same time learning Russian with the intention of emigrating to the Soviet Union. This he did in late 1959, being given a dishonourable discharge from the Marine Reserves as a result. Oswald lived in Russia from 1959 until June 1962, marrying a Russian girl, Marina Pruskova, in 1960. He re-emigrated to America in 1962, moved to the Dallas-Fort Worth area, and had a series of low-paying, dead-end jobs. During the week he lived apart from his wife, who roomed with a Quaker couple in suburban Dallas while Oswald lived in a cheap boarding house in Dallas itself. In 1963 Oswald did several other unusual things. In March, using the name A.J. Hidell, he purchased a mail-order rifle and revolver. . . .

In mid-1963 he went to New Orleans, where he founded a pro-Castro organisation, the "Fair Play for Cuba Committee," of which he was the only member. He also visited Mexico City with the aim of obtaining a Cuban visa from the Soviet embassy, but was rebuffed.

He returned to Dallas in early October completely demoralised, and began a poorly-paid warehouse job at the Texas School Book Depository Building in central Dallas. According to the Warren Report, at 12:30 PM on November 22, 1963, Oswald fired three shots from an upstairs window in that building at President Kennedy, riding by in an open limousine, seriously wounding both him and Texas Governor John Connally (riding in the same car) with the second shot and killing Kennedy with the third.

Oswald then fled from the Depository, returned to his boarding house and, at about 1:14 PM, shot and killed Dallas police officer J.D. Tippit, who had stopped Oswald as he was walking down the street. At 1:51 PM Oswald was arrested in a nearby movie theatre and charged with killing Tippit; he was later charged with the assassination of the President.

As he was being transferred to a normal jail, two days later, on the morning of Sunday, November 24, Oswald was shot and killed in the basement of the Dallas police headquarters by Jack Ruby (1911–67), a local nightclub owner. From a dysfunctional immigrant background, Ruby was a ne'er-do-well fringe businessman, pro-Kennedy but essentially apolitical, who killed Oswald, so he claimed, to spare Kennedy's widow Jacqueline the ordeal of having to testify at Oswald's trial. Ruby, who had swallowed many anti-depressant pills the previous day, was also in chronic financial difficulties. According to the Warren Report, Oswald and Ruby had never met.

Within days of the assassination, the new President, Lyndon Johnson, appointed a panel to investigate the killing. . . .

The Warren Commission Report

The Commission did a remarkable job and produced a twenty-seven volume report, containing around ten million words, by September 24th, 1964, only ten months

Conclusions of the Warren Commission

This Commission was created to ascertain the facts relating to the preceding summary of events and to consider the important questions they raised. The Commission has addressed itself to this task and has reached certain conclusions based on all the available evidence. No limitations have been placed on the Commission's inquiry; it has conducted its own investigation, and all Government agencies have fully discharged their responsibility to cooperate with the Commission in its investigation. These conclusions represent the reasoned judgment of all members of the Commission and are presented after an investigation which has satisfied the Commission that it: has ascertained the truth concerning the assassination of President Kennedy to the extent that a prolonged and thorough search makes this possible.

1. The shots which killed President [John F.] Kennedy and wounded Governor [John] Connally were fired from the sixth floor window at the southeast corner of the Texas School Book Depository. . . .
2. The weight of the evidence indicates that there were three shots fired.
3. Although it is not necessary to any essential findings of the Commission to determine just which shot hit Governor Connally, there is very persuasive evidence from the experts to indicate that the same bullet which pierced the President's throat also caused Governor Connally's wounds. However, Governor Connally's testimony and certain other factors have given rise to some difference of opinion as to this probability but there is no question in the mind of any member of the Commission that all the shots which caused the President's and Governor Connally's wounds were fired from the sixth floor window of the Texas School Book Depository.
4. The shots which killed President Kennedy and wounded Governor Connally were fired by Lee Harvey Oswald. . . .

after it had been appointed. On its behalf the FBI conducted 25,000 interviews, the Secret Service another 1,550. The Commission itself took testimony from 552 witnesses, of whom ninety-four appeared before it. The conclusions reached by the Warren Commission are

5. Oswald killed Dallas Police Patrolman J.D. Tippit approximately 45 minutes after the assassination. . . .
6. Within 80 minutes of the assassination and 35 minutes of the Tippit killing Oswald resisted arrest at the theatre by attempting to shoot another Dallas police officer. . . .
9. The Commission has found no evidence that either Lee Harvey Oswald or Jack Ruby was part of any conspiracy, domestic or foreign, to assassinate President Kennedy. . . .
10. In its entire investigation the Commission has found no evidence of conspiracy, subversion, or disloyalty to the U.S. Government by any Federal, State, or local official.
11. On the basis of the evidence before the Commission it concludes that Oswald acted alone. . . .
12. The Commission recognizes that the varied responsibilities of the President require that he make frequent trips to all parts of the United States and abroad. Consistent with their high responsibilities Presidents can never be protected from every potential threat. The Secret Service's difficulty in meeting its protective responsibility varies with the activities and the nature of the occupant of the Office of President and his willingness to conform to plans for his safety. In appraising the performance of the Secret Service it should be understood that it has to do its work within such limitations. Nevertheless, the Commission believes that recommendations for improvements in Presidential protection are compelled by the facts disclosed in this investigation. . . .

Source: *"Report of the President's Commission on the Assassination of President John F. Kennedy," 1964. The U.S. National Archives and Records Administration.*

well-known: Oswald assassinated President Kennedy, acting alone. There was no conspiracy of any kind. Oswald was in turn killed by Ruby, also acting alone; Oswald and Ruby had never met. Oswald fired three bullets: the first missed; the second, dubbed by critics the "magic bullet," hit Kennedy in the upper back, seriously wounding him, and then also hit John Connally, who sat in the same limousine two feet in front of the President, nearly killing him. The third and final bullet killed Kennedy by striking him in the right side of his head and blowing out a portion of his brain. All of the shots were fired within eight seconds or so from the Depository Building, and no one else was involved.

"There was much about the format of the Warren Commission to arouse suspicion and engender criticism."

Having discharged its functions, the Warren Commission disbanded. Even before it reported, however, there were already theories of conspiracies and within a few years the first books to criticise its findings appeared. There was much about the format of the Warren Commission to arouse suspicion and engender criticism. It was composed exclusively of Washington insiders. With the notable exception of Earl Warren, all of its members could be considered politically right-of-centre. None had any real expertise of such technical matters as ballistics or forensics. The involvement of former CIA director Allen Dulles as a Commission member, and the central role of the long-serving FBI director J. Edgar Hoover and his Agency in gathering information, was deeply suspicious to many. . . .

The fact that Kennedy's assassination seemed to signal a precipitous and disastrous change in America's Vietnam policy also seemed to many Warren critics to be more than coincidental. As both William Manchester and Gerald Posner have perceptively noted, to many it seemed inconceivable that so important an event as Kennedy's assassination could have been accomplished by a maladjusted loner with a mail-order rifle: surely so momentous an event required an equally far-reaching conspiracy? In part as a result, in the 1970s there was a fully-fledged subculture of Warren "critics" (as they are known), numbering hundreds. So great was the public outcry that in 1975 Congress held a second investigation. This had been given impetus by the notorious investigation conducted by New Orleans district attorney Jim Garrison in the late 1960s which claimed that three New Orleans-based anti-Castro right-wingers were behind the assassination. This claim (which is certainly nonsensical) received world-wide fame decades later as the basis for Oliver Stone's 1991 film *JFK*. Literally hundreds of books and articles have appeared by Warren critics. . . .

The case that Oswald did not kill Kennedy, or did not act alone, is superficially fairly strong.

Arguments Against the Official Explanation

The case that Oswald did not kill Kennedy, or did not act alone, is superficially fairly strong. There are some frequently reiterated points made by the Warren critics. Oswald had no motive: he never expressed hostility to Kennedy and made no political pronouncements when captured but said he was innocent: an unlikely stance if the killing had been politically motivated. Oswald's career as a U.S. Marine yet a Marxist who lived in Russia was so suspicious that it has seemed inconceivable to many that he was not a government agent or double agent. Some eyewitnesses (although, contrary to what is frequently said, only a minority) thought that some shots came from the "grassy knoll" in front of Kennedy's limousine. Any such shots must have come from a second assassin, and almost all "conspiracy theories" of the assassination revolve around the existence of a second or third gunman. The time-frame for the assassination is frequently seen as too narrow for Oswald to have fired all the shots. Many critics believe that Oswald lacked the time to run down from the sixth floor of the Depository before police arrived. Some argue that Oswald could not have walked from his boarding house and killed Tippit in the estimated time of twelve to fifteen minutes. Many claims have been made that evidence was tampered with, for instance the famous backyard photographs of Oswald holding the assassination rifle, taken by Marina Oswald on March 31, 1963. No direct transcript was made of Oswald's statements in custody, and at no time did he have a lawyer. Similarly, it has been argued by many critics that Ruby must have killed Oswald as part of a conspiracy. Critics point out that the Warren Report asks us to believe that Ruby just happened to enter the basement (carrying a loaded revolver) of the Dallas Police Headquarters at the precise moment that Oswald was being led through the basement, and managed to kill him from the front in full view of dozens of policemen and television cameramen. Ruby allegedly had links with organised crime figures. He claimed to be a Kennedy supporter, but had not bothered, two days previously, to see Kennedy drive by in the Dallas motorcade.

Given these suspicions surrounding the key participants in the assassination, it is not surprising that theory after theory has been posited since 1963 about the true nature of the killing. At least five major groupings of conspirators have been proposed over the years: a right-wing conspiracy within the American government, often including the CIA, J. Edgar Hoover, and Lyndon Johnson; a conspiracy of right-wing dissidents outside the government ("rogue" CIA agents, right-wing Texas oil magnate H.L. Hunt, international extreme right-wing groups); anti-Castro Cubans and their alleged supporters like Clay Shaw and David Ferrie; left-wing pro-Castro groups; and the Mafia, angry at Kennedy for launching a war against American organised crime. In some scenarios, members of these groups co-operated: for instance, the Mafia and anti-Castro Cubans (the Mafia had lost its lucrative casinos in Havana when Castro came to power in 1959). It is probably fair to say that the Mafia has emerged, in recent decades, as the leading candidate among conspiracy theorists as the group most likely to have carried out the assassination.

Reading the works produced by the Warren critics rapidly becomes a tedious business. There are such striking similarities in their approach, however much their theories differ, that the effect is like reading a detective novel from which the last ten pages have been torn out. There is circumstantial evidence in plenty, but nothing definite or clearly true beyond a reasonable doubt. In over thirty-five years of theorising on the assassination, no Warren critic has ever been able to provide cogent or convincing answers to the two most basic questions of any valid conspiracy theory: who masterminded it and what were the precise roles of Oswald and Ruby? No "smoking gun" has ever been traced, and the sheer plethora of theories clearly shows that the critics of the official explanation cannot agree among themselves.

It is undeniable that, by sheer weight of numbers, the critics have had a profound effect upon the public perception of the assassination.

Public Perception of the Assassination

Nevertheless, it is undeniable that, by sheer weight of numbers, the critics have had a profound effect upon the public perception of the assassination. By the late 1980s, polls showed that as many as 80 percent of the American public did not believe the Warren Commission, and did believe that others were involved besides Oswald. The critics held the field almost entirely to themselves until 1993, when Gerald Posner, a Wall Street lawyer and author of several previous works, published *Case Closed: Lee Harvey Oswald and the Assassination of JFK*, certainly the most important book ever written on the assassination. Posner became convinced that the Warren

Report was essentially correct in everything it asserted, and went over every Claim made by the Report's critics in elaborate detail, often with new evidence, refuting all of the claims made by the critics. For instance, critics have frequently claimed that over one hundred witnesses and others connected with the assassination have 'died mysteriously.' Posner examined every such alleged death and showed that not a single one was actually mysterious. . . .

Although Posner's book did not end the efforts of the Warren critics, which continue to appear in considerable numbers, *Case Closed* has probably changed the balance of public opinion on Kennedy's assassination in a significant way, so that a number of important studies of aspects of the assassination have appeared which also accept the findings of the Warren Report. . . .

Arguments Against the Conspiracy Theories

Indeed, it is possible to show, almost by the force of logic alone, that Oswald and Ruby must have acted as the Warren Report claimed. How did Oswald come to gain access to the sixth floor of the Depository building? He was found a job there purely by chance by a neighbour of the Paines (with whom Marina Oswald lodged) who worked there. No one has ever linked any of these persons with a conspiracy. Oswald was interviewed for the job and was hired because the superintendent of the Depository thought that he was unusually respectful. Oswald began working there on October 16, before Kennedy's trip to Texas was announced. The route of Kennedy's motorcade was not chosen until a week before the assassination, and not published until two days prior to the killing. Oswald could thus not have been planted ahead of time in the Depository Building by any conspirators.

Another key question is what inducement was offered to Oswald to kill the President. Oswald and his family were living in poverty. The Warren Commission examined Oswald's finances in detail and found that his income, between returning to America in June 1962 and the assassination, totalled only $3,666. (These findings have been ignored by all Warren critics.) He had earned no more than $225 in any of the five months prior to the killing. Would he not have demanded a huge upfront payment to kill the President? There are other basic questions as well: would the conspirators not have organised an escape route? If there was a second gunman in the Depository Building, why has no one ever claimed to see him?

The case that Ruby acted alone is even stronger. Ruby shot Oswald in an area containing seventy policemen and dozens of reporters. If Ruby was not shot dead on the spot (which was more than likely), he faced the absolute certainty of conviction for murder. No one in his right mind would agree to take part in a conspiracy to commit murder under these conditions. The first thing he would have demanded would be a guaranteed means of escape. Indeed, the first thing any conspirators would ensure would be an escape route for Ruby: otherwise, they might well merely have traded one conspirator in custody for another. Nor would any conspirators, for the absolutely crucial task of silencing Oswald, have used a middle-aged, low-life nightclub owner on anti-depressant pills with no real knowledge of guns. Any conspiracy would certainly have used a "professional killer" with a successful track record of murders. As with Oswald, there is no evidence of any kind that Ruby was offered any financial gain. Although there are indeed some curious loose ends in the Warren Commission's case, it does seem overwhelmingly likely

> [The amateur historians] are not open-mindedly searching for the objective truth, but argue from the premise that the Warren Report was wrong.

that Oswald and Ruby acted alone and that there was no conspiracy. . . .

A central aim of this article has been to examine how well the amateur historians have done. Not very well, although they have performed an extremely useful function by their dogged research and in compelling the American government to open its files for public inspection. The failure of the amateurs in this case has one main cause: they are not open-mindedly searching for the objective truth, but argue from the premise that the Warren Report was wrong. Since, however, the Commission's conclusions about the identity of the assassin and of the absence of a conspiracy are almost certainly correct, it is not surprising that the critics have been unable to identify a conspiracy in a convincing way. That no academic historian has ever examined Kennedy's assassination is a reproach to the historical profession. The training of academic historians in assessing evidence could hardly have been put to better or more important use, and this is one case in which academic historians should have left the ivory tower.

VIEWPOINT 3

Some Reputable Experts Believe the Assassination Involved Conspiracy

Jefferson Morley

In the following viewpoint, a journalist points out that while many theories about the Kennedy assassination are myths, so are some of the common assumptions about conspiracy theories. The idea of a gunshot from the "grassy knoll" came from reports of some people at the scene, for instance; it did not originate later. Belief in such theories is not confined to people with any particular political view. Some academic historians, scientists, and people of power in Washington reject the official account, and new information has been gained from the files released by public demand following the movie *JFK*. Jefferson Morley is a Washington, DC-based investigative journalist whose stories have appeared in many national publications and blogs. In 2006 he filed a lawsuit against the Central Intelligence Agency to force it to release certain documents related to the assassination; as of early 2010 the suit is still pending.

SOURCE. Jefferson Morley, "What JFK Conspiracy Bashers Get Wrong," *Huffington Post*, November 21, 2007. Reproduced by permission of the author.

As the 44th anniversary of the assassination of President John F. Kennedy approaches, you may get caught up in an eruption of the perennial and sometimes tedious conspiracy debate. You want to keep an open mind and make sure you don't fall for any JFK assassination myths. You can, for example, say with confidence that a lot of the crazy JFK conspiracy scenarios have been debunked over the years. No, neither the KGB, the Masons, the Mossad, nor the Red Chinese were behind the gunfire that killed the liberal statesman. No, Abraham Zapruder's famous home movie assassination was not secretly altered to hide evidence of a conspiracy. And, no, the legendary three tramps photographed that day did not whack Jack. They were just a trio of homeless guys in the wrong place at the wrong time.

> You can . . . say with confidence that a lot of the crazy JFK conspiracy scenarios have been debunked over the years.

But no sooner were these fables dispatched by scrupulous JFK researchers, than public discourse on the JFK story was engulfed by a new set of assertions imbued with an anti-conspiratorial animus that is also unhinged from the historical record. These too need the truth squad treatment.

Myth #1: JFK conspiratorial suspicions, like the idea of a gunshot from the so-called grassy knoll, were ginned up after the fact by demagogues like Oliver Stone.

In fact, a significant minority of eyewitnesses at the scene of the crime thought at least one of the gunshots that hit Kennedy came from the knoll, which was actually a grassy embankment bordering a parking lot overlooking the route of JFK's motorcade through downtown Dallas. A survey of eyewitness statements, compiled by conspiracy skeptic John McAdams of Marquette University, found that 42 of 103 bystanders said that the gunfire

The Texas School Book Depository (left) dominates Dealey Plaza in Dallas. The so-called grassy knoll is visible to the left. (AP Images.)

came from the knoll or from two different directions. To be sure, a larger number said that shots came from a high window of the Texas School Book Depository. And, yes, the parking lot on the knoll was searched within minutes and no gunman or ballistic debris was found. And, yes, ear witness testimony is notoriously unreliable.

The fact remains that more than 30 people in the vicinity of Kennedy's limousine—including Dallas sheriff Bill Decker, Secret Service agent Roy Kellerman and presidential aide David Powers—independently said that they thought a gunshot came from the knoll. Within a week of the crime, pollsters found 62 percent of respondents nationwide said they thought two or more people were responsible. In Dallas, the figure was 66 percent.

Myth #2: JFK conspiracy theories are mostly held by anti-American leftists and credulous liberals.

Try telling that to Bruce Willis. "They still haven't caught the guy that killed [President] Kennedy," the leading Republican in Hollywood told *Vanity Fair* last spring [2007]. Willis was merely voicing a view that has long circulated on the American right. In September 1964, Warren Commission member Senator Richard Russell, a paleoconservative from Georgia, rejected the so-called single bullet theory and attempted to put a dissent into the commission's final report (only to be slapped down by liberal Chief Justice Earl Warren). By the late 1960s, conservative figures ranging from former congresswoman Clare Booth Luce to columnist William F. Buckley to Nixon White House chief of staff H.R. Haldeman dissented publicly or privately from the Warren report. Mary Ferrell, one of the best-informed JFK researchers, was so adamantly opposed to legal abortion that she told friends that she never voted for a Democrat after 1980. Today, the best JFK assassination Web site, MaryFerrell.org, is named after her.

Myth #3: No reputable historian believes in a JFK conspiracy.

Wrong. I know of four tenured academic historians who have written directly on the JFK assassination in the past five years. Three of them (Gerald McKnight of Hood College, David Wrone of the University of Wisconsin-Steven Points, Michael Kurtz of Southeast Louisiana University) came to conspiratorial conclusions, while one (Robert Dallek of UCLA) vouched for the lone gunman theory. A forthcoming book by Naval War College historian David Kaiser on Kennedy's Cuba policy and the assassination, to be published by Harvard University Press next year [actually released in 2009], is likely to demolish this myth once and for all. (Full disclosure: Kaiser is a friend and the book will cite my JFK reporting.)

Myth #4: Serious people of power in Washington overwhelmingly believe there was no conspiracy.

Hardly. The slain president's own brother Bobby Kennedy was, in the words of journalist David Talbot, "America's first conspiracy theorist." He and First Lady Jackie Kennedy quickly concluded that JFK was the victim of a major domestic plot. Lyndon Johnson suspected that the assassination resulted from the struggle for power in Cuba. Richard Nixon hounded the CIA for files on "the whole Bay of Pigs thing," which his aides understood to mean Kennedy's assassination. George H.W. Bush, upon becoming CIA director in 1976, immediately asked for the JFK assassination file, not exactly the action of someone who thought he knew the whole story. Bill Clinton and Al Gore both said publicly in 1992 that they believed there had been a conspiracy. (Once in office, Clinton recanted.) George W. Bush, to be sure, is a firm believer in the lone nut theory. But, when it comes to providing credible explanations of U.S. intelligence failures that culminated in national catastrophe, Bush's track record is not reassuring.

Myth #5: Scientists unequivocally support the lone gunman theory.

The latest peer-reviewed articles indicate otherwise. One piece of scientific analysis, "bullet lead analysis," that was long used to buttress the so-called "single bullet" theory has been decisively debunked, as a recent front page series in the *Washington Post* shows. A study of the JFK ballistics evidence, published in the *Journal of Forensic Science* in 2006, concluded that its findings "considerably weaken support for the single-bullet theory." A pair of articles on the medical evidence, published in *Neurosurgery* in 2004, offered a split decision. One supported the official story; the other provided strong evidence based on sworn testimony from multiple eyewitnesses that the photographic record of JFK's autopsy has been

Was There a Cover-up?

Most people, even those who agree with the Warren Commission's conclusions, believe that its report did not contain all the facts about John F. Kennedy's assassination. And, in fact, a congressional committee stated in the 1976 Schweiker-Hart Report that "the investigation of the assassination was deficient" and that the FBI and CIA withheld information from the commission. In 1979 the House Select Committee on Assassinations (HSCA), which conducted a more thorough inquiry, reported that Kennedy was "probably killed as a result of a conspiracy" without indicating who was involved, and it was later found that information had been withheld from that committee, too.

The majority of Americans are convinced that there could be no legitimate reason for hiding any information and that government corruption of one sort or another must have been involved. An article published at the Web site of the Mary Ferrell Foundation, an organization that has assembled a vast collection of documents and commentary about the assassination, offers another explanation. "The declassification of tapes of Lyndon Johnson's phone calls, along with other documents, provided an explanation for why the Warren Commission might have engaged in a cover-up: to prevent World War III. Johnson continually refers in phone calls to 'foreign complications' (allegations of Communist conspiracy, mainly emanating from Mexico City) and that the lives of '40 million Americans' were at stake." If anyone alive knows what Johnson meant, it has not been made public—but the President of the United States has access to information affecting national security that few other officials possess.

tampered with. The acoustic evidence—a Dallas Police Department radio recording that some scientists say contains evidence of a shot from the grassy knoll—has been called into question but not refuted by other scientists. The issue remains unresolved. My own review of the crime scene evidence, published this month [November 2007] on Playboy.com, concludes that the scientific case for Oswald's sole guilt has been weakened in recent years.

A handful of top CIA officials had much greater knowledge of Oswald's travels and political activities in the weeks before Kennedy was killed than they ever let on.

Myth #6: There is nothing significant to be found in the new JFK files identified since Oliver Stone's JFK.

Depends on how closely you care to look. The long suppressed CIA records made public since the 1990s certainly do not confirm Stone's depiction of the assassination as a virtual *coup d'etat* by the CIA and the Pentagon, but they do raise new questions about the Dallas tragedy. They demonstrate that a handful of top CIA officials had much greater knowledge of Oswald's travels and political activities in the weeks before Kennedy was killed than they ever let on. At least one of these operatives—an undercover officer named George Joannides—remained quiet about what he knew of Oswald's Cuban contacts to perhaps a criminal extent.

As I reported in the Huffington Post, CIA attorneys appeared in federal court last month [October 2007] seeking to block the release of dozens of secret records on Joannides's actions in 1963. At the time, Joannides served in Miami as the chief of psychological warfare operations aimed at overthrowing Fidel Castro. The CIA argues that release of any portion of more than 30 documents about Joannides—some of them 45 years old—would harm U.S. national security and foreign policy in 2007. Don't take my word that these records are significant. Just ask the CIA's lawyers.

When you strip away all the tall tales of JFK's assassination, the unsatisfying and infuriating truth is that we still don't have the full story. And that's no myth.

VIEWPOINT 4

Reports of Eyewitnesses Do Not Fit the Belief in a Single Assassin

Ralph Schuster

Conspiracy theories about the assassination of John F. Kennedy are common in Europe. The following viewpoint from a German Web site summarizes what witnesses reported, concluding that the Warren Commission report is not accurate and that the fact that many of those witnesses have died suddenly raises concerns. It then summarizes the main conspiracy theories and explains the investigation by New Orleans district attorney Jim Garrison, which is considered by many to be one of the most important. Finally, it argues that the CIA had motives for assassinating Kennedy. Ralph Schuster is an information technology manager in Frankfurt, Germany. He first created a Web site about the assassination in 1996, and his current site, the John F. Kennedy Assassination Homepage, contains an extensive index of research materials.

SOURCE. Ralph Schuster, "The Assassination: An Overview and Frequently Asked Questions," *The John F. Kennedy Assassination Homepage*, March 4, 2006. Reproduced by permission.

During his electoral battle tour in the south of the [United] States, John F. Kennedy visited Dallas (Texas) on November 22, 1963. On his arrival at 11:40, he was warmly welcomed by the people of Dallas. Kennedy, Governor John Connally and their wives sat down in the limousine of the President which led the motorcade through the town.

When the motorcade arrived in Dealey Plaza at 12:30, it turned right from Main to Houston Street and just seconds later it took the 120 degree turn onto Elm Street, passing the School Book Depository Building.

Just when the limousine passed the Stemmons Freeway sign, Mrs. Connally heard gunshots. When she turned looking at the President, she saw him taking his hand to his throat covering a shooting wound. The next second Governor Connally felt an ache in his back, which he recognized as a shot. He later said: "There were either two or three people involved or more in this or someone was shooting with an automatic rifle."

Just seconds later he could hear the third shot. Mrs. Kennedy, who then believed she listened to firecrackers from the motorcade, heard at this moment "terrible noises" and turned to Kennedy. She saw her husband being wounded by a head shot. This was the last and final, fatal shot at Dealey Plaza.

The reaction of the Secret Service Agents was quite slow. Most of them spent the evening before in "The Cellar" bar that was owned by an acquaintance of Jack Ruby.

Forty-five minutes later, Lee Harvey Oswald was arrested on a charge of murder of police officer J.D. Tippit. After hours of interrogation where no lawyer was present and no protocol was followed, Oswald was accused of the murder of John F. Kennedy. On November 24, 1963, a Sunday morning, he was supposed to be handed over to the State Prison. In the garage of the police building, he was shot by Jack Ruby in front of hundreds of journalists and millions of television watchers.

The Warren Commission—constituted one week later—declared after months of investigation:

1. Lee Harvey Oswald was the only assassin and acted on his own.
2. He shot from the 6th floor of the School Book Depository Building, which was behind the President's limousine at the time of the assassination.
3. He used the found Italian Mannlicher-Carcano rifle.
4. Oswald shot police officer Tippit.

Evidence Against the Warren Commission's Conclusions

The crowd of witnesses in Dealey Plaza saw things differently from this official version of the Warren Commission, e.g.:

1. Many witnesses reported that shots were fired from the Grassy Knoll, not the Texas School Book Depository.
2. Witnesses stated that a cloud of smoke was visible in the area of the Grassy Knoll.
3. Even before the motorcade arrived, men with rifles were seen by people in downtown Dallas.
4. There were unexplained reports of witnesses encountering mysterious Secret Service men in Dealey Plaza.

> Dallas Police Chief Jesse Curry admitted to newsmen: 'We don't have any proof that Oswald fired the rifle, and never did.'

In later years, Dallas Police Chief Jesse Curry admitted to newsmen: "We don't have any proof that Oswald fired the rifle, and never did. Nobody's yet been able to put him in that building with a gun in his hand."

Oswald told Dallas Police he was eating lunch on the first floor of the Depository in what was called the "Domino Room" at the time of the assassination, and there is some evidence to back up his statement.

The third wounded man doesn't fit into the version of the Warren Commission, too: James Tague. He stood near the Triple Underpass ahead of the motorcade and was wounded by a passing bullet. Because the first shot wounded Kennedy's throat, the second Connally's back, and the third was the head shot, there must had been a fourth shot. This made the Warren Commission change their version and create the "Magic Bullet" theory. This bullet was supposed to cause the seven wounds of Kennedy and Connally. This Commission Exhibit #399 was found later in an almost pristine condition (!) at Parkland Memorial.

> In the three-year period which followed the murders of President Kennedy and Lee Harvey Oswald, eighteen material witnesses died.

One of the most known pieces of evidence is the film which Abraham Zapruder took directly next to the Grassy Knoll that day. It shows the assassination in full length. There, one can also see the opened umbrella of the Umbrella Man despite the shining sun and cloudless sky.

More photos show two suspicious men behind the fence at the Grassy Knoll—one with a rifle—who have been called "Black Dog Man" and "Badge Man" because of their unknown identity. The Warren Commission never mentioned these men and never made any effort to find them.

In the three-year period which followed the murders of President Kennedy and Lee Harvey Oswald, eighteen material witnesses died—six by gunfire, three in motor accidents, two by suicide, one from a cut throat, one from a karate chop to the neck, three from heart attacks and two from natural causes. In the late 1970s, the House Select Committee on Assassinations [HSCA] felt compelled to look into the matter. The Committee was unable to come to any conclusion regarding the growing number of deaths. However, an objective look at both the number and the causes of death, balanced against the importance of the person's connection to the case, raises concern. . . .

If It Was a Conspiracy, Who Was Responsible?

The conspiracy theories are very extensive. So I will shortly introduce them to you:

- Government agencies did it. The assassination was planned by high officials in the White House, Secret Service, FBI and CIA. It was executed by paid killers. Most probably the order was sent to the Mob and they did it. Afterwards the agencies ensured that the murderers remained undiscovered.
- The Mafia did it. The Mob planned and executed the assassination. Indication is the involvement of Jack Ruby who had connections to the Mafia.
- Right wing extremists did it. For them, Kennedy was Communist as he tried to build peaceful relationships with Cuba and the Soviet Union. So they planned and executed the assassination.
- Communists did it. The Communists saw in Kennedy a friend of industrialists and responsible for the war in Vietnam, the blockade against Cuba and many other things. So they decided to kill him.

Beside that, there are minor theories. But they are not relevant here and have almost no basis at all.

Is There Any Substance to the Garrison Investigation?

Before I can answer the question, let me give a short overview of the investigation. In November 1963, Jim Gar-

Millions saw Jack Ruby (right) kill accused assassin Lee Harvey Oswald in a televised press conference. Witnesses to Kennedy's death were far fewer and held variant interpretations of that murder. **(Popperfoto/Getty Images.)**

rison (District Attorney of New Orleans then) learned by a television report that Oswald spent the summer of 1963 in New Orleans. Often he (Oswald) was seen with David W. Ferrie, who participated in the 1961 Bay of Pigs invasion. Garrison arrested Ferrie because he gave him a very unbelievable story of his activities on November 22. After he turned Ferrie over to the FBI, they released him shortly after with a complete clearing of any involvement in the assassination. Ferrie died in 1967. That was just a few days after the public had learned of the investigation which Garrison re-started in 1966. Ferrie was his best witness that time. In the investigation, the name Clay Bertrand turned up again and again as a business associate of Ferrie. Clay Bertrand was the alias of Clay Shaw. Under the name Bertrand, Shaw hired an attorney (Dean Andrews) to defend Oswald.

Garrison charged Shaw, but he was not [found] guilty. Although Garrison proved that a conspiracy did exist, the jury saw no evidence that connected Shaw to it.

Afterwards the Government agencies tried multiple times to silence Garrison. He was prosecuted a couple of times, but both times he could prove very clearly that all the charges against him were groundless, completely false and . . . [manufactured] by FBI and CIA.

In his book, Garrison wrote: "Considering the lofty credentials of the Commission members and the quality and size of the staff available to them, I had expected to find a thorough and professional investigation. I found nothing of the sort. The mass of information was disorganized and confused. The Commission had provided no adequate index to its exhibits. . . . The number of promising leads that were never followed up offended my prosecutorial sensibility. And, perhaps worst of all, the conclusions in the Report seemed to be based on an appallingly selective reading of the evidence, ignoring credible testimony from literally dozens of witnesses."

A Deeper Look at the Investigation

Okay, now let's take a deeper look into his investigation.

In summer 1963, Oswald had distributed leaflets for the "Fair Play for Cuba Committee." On these leaflets, there was a stamp with the address of the Committee's office at 544 Camp Street, New Orleans. This building had two entrances—first is 544 Camp Street, second is 531 Lafayette Street, the office of Guy Banister. Banister was a leading member of the Anti-Communist League of the Caribbean. That leads us to the confusion between

Oswald and Banister. Oswald was not a Communist. He most probably was framed to be one. Because of the suspicious activities in that building, it is most likely that Oswald, Ferrie, Banister, Anti-Cubans and weapon dealers were deeply connected to each other.

During the court trial against Shaw, Garrison called Dr. Pierre Finck . . . to testify. "Finck informed the court that some powerful, high-ranking officers had kept him (and the other attending physicians) from performing the autopsy in accordance with proper military procedure. Finck also stated for the court that the bullet that had caused the wound in the President's back did not pass through his body. . . . Garrison's team presented evidence proving the single bullet theory invalid."

> [Jim Garrison's] theory that CIA, FBI, Secret Service and high officials in the White House did conspire to kill Kennedy is now one of the most consistent and most accepted theories among the researchers.

At the trial, Shaw testified that he did not know—and never met—Ferrie. But there are photographs which show him and Ferrie together at parties.

Garrison revealed another witness, Perry Russo, who testified that in September 1963 he was at a gathering in Ferrie's apartment where he overheard Shaw discussing the Kennedy assassination. He discovered major discrepancies in the story of Oswald's activities in Russia. Oswald could not have taken a scheduled flight to Russia. And although Oswald had betrayed military secrets (an Air Force plane crash over Russia most likely could be done only by his help), he got back [his] American citizenship . . . without questions or difficulties. The State Department even gave him a loan to come back.

Jim Garrison was one of the most important researchers that the case ever had. . . . His theory that CIA, FBI, Secret Service and high officials in the White House did conspire to kill Kennedy is now one of the most consistent and most accepted theories among the researchers. Even those who do not share his idea cannot ignore him and have to agree at least partially.

Jim Marrs wrote about him: "Even today many assassination researchers—particularly those who pay closest attention to Government officials and fail to take the trouble to dig deep into the New Orleans investigation—believe Garrison was far afield of truth about Kennedy's death . . . it is now obvious that a concerted effort was made by elements within the Federal Government and the national news media to discredit his evidence and destroy his reputation even before he had a chance to bring his case to court." . . .

Did the CIA Have Anything to Do with the Assassination?

An indication that the CIA did pay Oswald or at least that he was a major help for them are Oswald's employments at various CIA firms or firms which were deeply connected to the CIA.

Why did the CIA help in killing their own President? Let's remember some important facts of that time:

Kennedy denied the CIA any help in the Bay of Pigs invasion. One of the biggest factors that led to the end of the Cuba crisis was Kennedy's assurance that the USA would not invade Cuba. This decision had been a severe blow to the CIA. They trained exiled Cubans in camps in Louisiana and Florida just for that very purpose.

The CIA had planned and executed dozens of "covert operations" since the 1950s. These operations did make up more than 30 percent of their activities at that time. They did develop and distribute propaganda material, rob secret armies, stage *coup d'etats* and even murders all around the world. In 1975, a Senate Committee discovered under Frank Church that the agency planned many assassinations with the help of different poisons, automatic rifles and even Mafia killers. . . .

But Kennedy set other policies during his Presidency: He denied Air Force help for the invasion in Cuba (Bay of Pigs), declined the suggestion to drop bombs on Cuba and to occupy it during the missile crisis, and signed memorandums to withdraw from Vietnam in 1963. The reason why Kennedy was killed is obvious from the actions by the new Government after the assassination. The decision to withdraw from Vietnam was rolled back, the incident in the Gulf of Tonkin in August 1964 smelled of the CIA's involvement (on August 7, 1964, Johnson advised to take all military steps to secure the Americans—a de facto war declaration). When the United States finally signed the Treaty of Paris, 75,000 Americans and millions of Vietnam people died in that war.

Kennedy had enemies in the highest circles of the CIA and FBI.

Kennedy had enemies in the highest circles of the CIA and FBI. He fired the Chief Executive of the CIA, Charles Cabell. Among his enemies were Richard Helms and former CIA director Allen Dulles (a member of the Warren Commission!!!), Gerald Ford (who leaked information to the FBI during the Warren investigation).

George [H.W.] Bush tried to cover up all CIA actions regarding the assassination. In 1976, when the HSCA conducted its investigation, he called a meeting with CBS [television] officials William Paley and Richard Salant to gain support for the CIA's policy of "burying the past." When dealing with CIA contacts within the CBS, one told Bush, "we protect ours, you protect yours." Robert J. Groden writes about Bush: "The President John F. Kennedy Act of 1992 was enacted as a result of public outcry following the release of the movie *JFK*. The Act requires any federal agency holding unreleased documents relating to the assassination to catalogue and transfer them to the National Archives. By June 1993, this review body still had not been appointed, partly because former President (and CIA director) George Bush left office with the needed records in his possession."

VIEWPOINT 5

Conspiracy Theories Have Been Based on Faulty Research

Massimo Polidoro

In the following viewpoint, Italian researcher Massimo Polidoro argues that theories about the Kennedy assassination have been based on faulty research and unfounded conclusions. Eyewitness testimony is unreliable, he says, because perception and memory are not always accurate and witnesses can unintentionally provide false information. For example, a well-known witness in the Kennedy case related details that do not match what pictures show. Furthermore, self-styled experts have declared that a single bullet would have to follow a zigzag path to produce the injuries sustained by both President Kennedy and Governor Connally. He argues that, if their positions in the car are considered, it can be seen that a straight bullet trajectory would do so and that the only place from which such a

---

SOURCE. Massimo Polidoro, "Facts and Fiction in the Kennedy Assassination: Notes on a Strange World," *Skeptical Inquirer*, January–February 2005.

bullet could have been fired was the sixth floor of the Texas School Book Depository. Massimo Polidoro is a psychologist and the author of many books. He is the executive director of CICAP, the Italian Committee for the Investigation of Claims of the Paranormal. This article was adapted from his presentation at the 2004 World Skeptics Congress in Abano Terme, Italy.

Investigating historical mysteries is, possibly, one of the most fascinating and rewarding aspects of the work of a skeptical researcher. Mysteries that appear to have no possible solutions, that could certainly be termed "cold," can, sometimes, become clearer thanks to a more careful investigation of the original sources and also to the advancements of science. . . .

> Eyewitness testimonies and self-styled experts, even in good faith, can alter details and hide important clues that—if untouched—could lead to radically different conclusions.

However, cases are often made more difficult to solve when facts get confused with imagined realities and unfounded conclusions. Eyewitness testimonies and self-styled experts, even in good faith, can alter details and hide important clues that—if untouched—could lead to radically different conclusions. In order to give you some clear examples of what I mean, I will examine one of the great tragedies of the twentieth century. . . .

The Day JFK Died

Let's get back to that fatal day, November 22, 1963. President [John F.] Kennedy arrived in Dallas, Texas, during the election campaign. In 1964, there would have been new elections, and Kennedy, who wanted to be sure to be re-elected, had started a tour of the southern states, the most conservative ones, where he was less popular due to his progressive ideas.

The Zapruder Film

As the presidential motorcade passed through Dealey Plaza in Dallas, Texas, Abraham Zapruder, a private citizen, was filming it with a home movie camera. Though only 26.6 seconds long, his silent footage—which captured the moment when President Kennedy was hit—has become one of the most famous films ever made.

Realizing that he had something of potential significance, Zapruder gave two copies to the Secret Service but sold the original and the print rights to *Life* magazine, which published frames from it in black and white and later in color. The film was studied extensively by the Warren Commission and other investigators but was not seen by the general public until 1975, when a showing on the television program *Good Night America* led to outraged demands for congressional investigation of details that appeared to conflict with the commission's conclusions. These demands resulted in the Schweiker-Hart hearings and, ultimate-

It was decided that a motorcade would be conducted through the city. Kennedy and his wife would be in the backseat of the presidential limousine, and Governor [John] Connally and his wife would sit in front of them.

Dealey Plaza, in downtown Dallas, is a large, basin-like square where three roads converge toward an underpass that leads to a freeway. The Presidential limousine entered the plaza, moved slowly along Houston Street, then took a left turn right in front of the Texas School Book Depository building.

It was thirty minutes past noon. What happened next was documented by a movie buff, Abraham Zapruder, who was filming the motorcade with an 8 mm movie camera. The film is silent, for there was no audio on home-movie cameras back then. During the shocking sequence, the President can be seen waving to the crowd, but then he is hit by something and brings his hands

ly, the formation of the House Select Committee on Assassinations (HSCA).

The film, which is shocking and graphic, is widely believed by conspiracy theorists to provide evidence that there was more than one gunman. However, different observers have offered different interpretations of the head movements it shows, and no definite conclusions can be reached from it. Also, some copies have missing frames.

After considerable litigation and negotiation about rights, the film was returned by *Life* to the Zapruder family and later, under the John F. Kennedy Records Collection Act of 1992, the original was seized by the government, which paid the family $16 million as compensation. It is now stored in the National Archives, but copies can be seen on YouTube and elsewhere on the Internet. The copyright was donated by the family to the Sixth Floor Museum at the Texas School Book Depository in Dallas.

to his neck, right in front of him. Governor Connally starts to turn and shake; he is hit as well. Then, there is a fatal shot to Kennedy's head. He died soon after at the hospital.

Who killed him? It was soon determined that the shots came from the sixth floor of the Book Depository. There, piles of boxes were found, stashed around a window, creating a "sniper's nest" with a clear view of the site of the shooting. A rifle was also found that had just been fired along with three spent cartridge shells.

After about two hours, a suspect was stopped. He had had a confrontation with the police inside a movie theater, and it was later found out that he had just shot dead a policeman who had stopped him on a nearby street.

His name was Lee Harvey Oswald; he was a young man who worked at the depository and had been seen on the sixth floor of that building just minutes before the shooting. After that, he disappeared, and he turned out to be the only employee absent from the depository for no legitimate reason.

Oswald was an ex-marine and Communist sympathizer. The evidence against him quickly piled up, but only three days after his capture, during his transfer to a police van that would escort him to a more secure prison, nightclub owner Jack Ruby shot him dead.

Those of you who have seen the Oliver Stone movie *JFK*, where this story is told in great detail, will remember the many contradictions coming out of the official investigation of the assassination. I have seen that movie as well, and, like anyone else, I couldn't help but be convinced that Oswald could not be the only assassin. There had to be more than one killer, and this meant that there had been a conspiracy plot to kill the president.

At least, I believed that until I started to research the story for my latest book, and the strangest thing to me was that the deeper I went into it, the more the Oliver Stone version of the story looked weirder and weirder.

I can't go into the countless details here, as I have done in the book, but I'll give you just a couple of examples of the kind of pitfalls into which a historical investigator can easily fall.

I Saw It; I Was There . . .

Most strange phenomena and conspiracy theories rely on eyewitness testimony. Psychologists are aware of the many limits of memory and perception—and the fallibility of eyewitness accounts.

One of the best-known witnesses to the assassination, and the only one who is also the author of a book from the point of view of an eyewitness, was a woman named Jean Hill. She can be seen in the Zapruder film, standing beside a friend.

In her testimony, told and retold over the last forty years, she claimed among other things that she was looking at the limousine where she saw Kennedy and his wife,

Jackie; the couple was "looking at a little dog between them," a "white fluffy dog." Hill then jumped to the edge of the street to yell, "Hey, we want to take your picture!" JFK turned over to look at her. At that point, he was shot, and Jackie shouted, "My God, he has been shot!" Then, Mrs. Hill said that she saw "some men in plain clothes shooting back" and "a man with a hat running toward the monument" on the other side of the plaza on the so-called "grassy knoll." Immediately, she started running after him, thinking he was involved in the shooting. "When I ran across the street," she specified, "the first motorcycle that was right behind the President's car nearly hit me."

Thus, she was the first person to run up the grassy knoll, and many followed her. However, the man ran off and she missed him. She was convinced that this man was Jack Ruby, the club owner who, in three days, would kill Lee Harvey Oswald.

And there we have our proof for the existence of a conspiracy.

This, however, is one of those rare occasions in which dozens of reporters and photographers are present on the scene of an event and so there are countless statements on record from eyewitnesses and pictures from every angle. Thus, we can compare Jean Hill's memory with actual facts.

- She said that she was looking at the limousine.

  In the film, you can see that when Kennedy is shot the first time, she is looking away from him.

- She said that the couple was "looking at a little dog between them," a "white fluffy dog."

  There was no dog between them, just a bunch of red flowers.

- She said that she "jumped to the edge of the street"

The view from the sixth floor of the Texas School Book Depository shows that the bullet that hit both President Kennedy and Texas governor John Connally could only have come from here. **(CBS Photo Archive/Getty Images.)**

to yell, "Hey, we want to take your picture!" and JFK turned over to look at her.

The Zapruder film shows that Hill never moved or said a word—and the President did not turn to look over. In fact, he had just been shot when he passed in front of her.

- She said that Jackie shouted, "My God, he has been shot!"

Jackie and the car's four other witnesses deny that Jackie said anything.

- She said that she saw "some men in plain clothes shooting back."

But in an interview recorded just forty minutes after the assassination by a Dallas television station, she was asked: "Did you see the person who fired the—" and she answered: "No . . . I didn't see any person fire the weapon . . . I only heard it."

- She said that she immediately started running after the "man with a hat," thinking he was involved in the shooting. "When I ran across the street," she specified, "the first motorcycle that was right behind the President's car nearly hit me."

  But as can be seen in the many pictures taken during those fatal moments, she stands still at her place as the limousine and the motorbikes pass by. She even sits on the grass while all of the cars of the motorcade proceed behind the President's limousine.

- She also specified that after jumping into the middle of the road, she was the first person to run up the grassy knoll, and many followed her.

  In photographs, you can see a lot of people running around the area and up to the grassy knoll, but Hill always stays in the same spot, probably shocked by the whole thing, like most of the people present.

- She was convinced that the man she had followed was Jack Ruby.

  At that precise moment, Ruby was witnessed by many to be at the offices of the Dallas Morning News.

> It is quite clear what happens to some people when they find themselves right in the middle of history and have absolutely no role in it. They imagine one.

Now, as we can see, facts contradict many details of Jean Hill's dramatic testimony. Aside from excusable mistakes and errors made in good faith, we have here a story that, over the years, has changed and grown out of proportion, to the point that Mrs. Hill became a sort of celebrity, invited to every meeting of JFK buffs, and was even depicted in

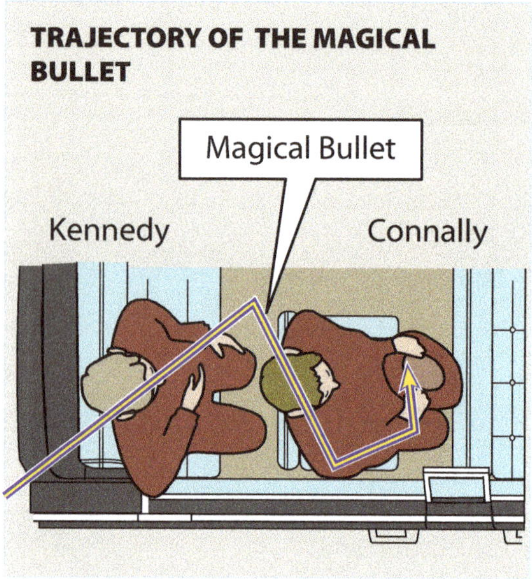

Figure 1

Oliver Stone's movie. She is the proud holder of a card bragging that she was the "closest witness" to the President at the time of the fatal shot to the head. It is quite clear what happens to some people when they find themselves right in the middle of history and have absolutely no role in it. They imagine one.

This Must Be So; I Know . . .

Imagined testimonies are just one of the many problems that an investigator of historical mysteries has to deal with. Another one is "imagined experts," that is, self-styled experts with no real expertise in the chosen field except what they think is "common sense." The Kennedy assassination presents dozens of such cases, but one of the most popular involves the so-called "magic bullet."

> From the analysis performed by real experts, it turns out that there was only one position from which this bullet could be shot.

The Warren Commission that investigated the Kennedy assassination concluded that the reactions of Kennedy and Connally occurred too close together for two separate shots, even from the same gun, to have been responsible for their wounds. They almost seem to react at the same instant, in the enhanced version of the film seen by the commission. They concluded that one, single bullet caused the injuries to both the President and the Governor.

This is where the "imagined experts" step in and say: "It must have been a really magical bullet in order to enter Kennedy from the back, exit from his throat, then make a turn and enter Connally's back, exit from his chest, hit his right wrist, make another bend, and, finally, land in his left thigh!" How could a single bullet follow this zigzag route, seen in Figure 1 [shown at left]?

Their conclusion is obvious: those injuries could not have been produced by just one bullet, so there had to be more than one shooter—further proof of a conspiracy.

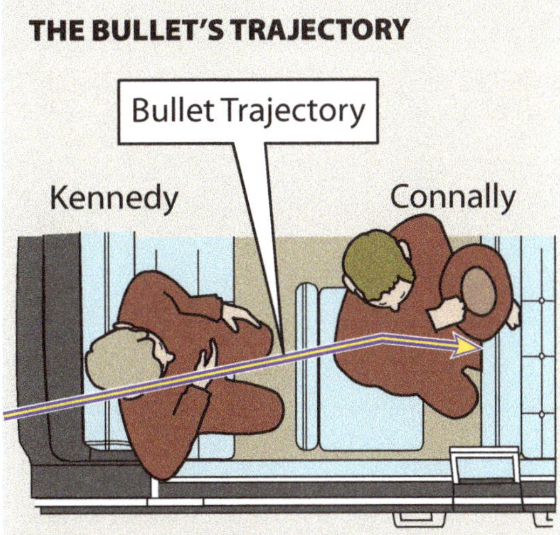

Taken From: Massimo Polidoro, "Facts and Fiction in the Kennedy Assassination," *Skeptical Inquirer*, January-February 2005.

Figure 2

This conclusion, however, as logical as it may sound at first, does not take real facts into account. And it only works until you don't look at Kennedy's and Connally's actual positions in the car. They were not one in front of the other; Kennedy was in a higher position in the back seat, and Connally was sitting lower, in the middle of the front seat of the car. So, in order to produce those injuries, the path shown in Figure 2 [above] is the real trajectory that a bullet had to follow, and, from the analysis performed by real experts, it turns out that there was only one position from which this bullet could be shot: the sixth floor of the Texas School Book Depository.

What can we conclude from these examples? Certainly that investigators must guard against preconceived ideas before starting an investigation. Before you know it, you start twisting facts and discarding evidence that contradicts those ideas, making you draw unfounded solutions. What we should do instead is to try to do our best to dig up facts and let them speak for themselves. They may have things to say that often turn out to be quite surprising.

VIEWPOINT 6

A Former Communist Official Says the Soviets Arranged the Assassination

Jeffrey R. Nyquist

The following viewpoint explains the opinion of Ion Mihai Pacepa, the former chief of Communist Romania's foreign intelligence service. He believes that the Soviet intelligence agency KGB arranged to have John F. Kennedy killed and that Lee Harvey Oswald was a Soviet agent. According to Pacepa's book, *Programmed to Kill*, there is considerable evidence that he might have been. Moreover, Soviet premier Nikita Khrushchev had reason to hate Kennedy, and Pacepa's superiors in Romanian intelligence thought he intended to kill him. Pacepa also believes the Soviets spread the story that the CIA assassinated Kennedy to divert attention away from themselves. The viewpoint's author, Jeffrey Nyquist, says that the Americans should read Pacepa's book and judge for themselves. Jeffrey R.

SOURCE. Jeffrey R. Nyquist, "Politics by Assassination?" FinancialSense.com, August 1, 2008.

Nyquist is an online conservative political columnist, author, and radio show host.

Did the Kremlin order a hit on President John F. Kennedy . . . ? The former chief of Communist Romania's foreign intelligence service thinks so. And he lays out his case in a recently [2008] published book with the title *Programmed to Kill: Lee Harvey Oswald, the Soviet KGB, and the Kennedy Assassination*. According to Ion Mihai Pacepa, "all Soviet-bloc espionage services were identically organized and had an identical modus operandi." Pacepa also explained that, "Soviet espionage operations . . . can easily be identified by their particular patterns, if you are familiar with them."

Looking at the case of Lee Harvey Oswald, Pacepa sees a KGB pattern. In the mid-to-late 1950s the Soviet bloc intelligence services were ordered to recruit American servicemen. To this end, loose women were used as "spotters" at bars and nightclubs located near U.S. military bases in Germany and Japan. They were told to watch for U.S. servicemen sympathetic to left-liberal or Marxist ideas. Lee Harvey Oswald was not only an America serviceman stationed in Japan in 1957, he was fascinated by Marxism. As a Marine Corps radar operator, Oswald also possessed clues to the flight altitude of the American U-2 spy plane. It was no accident, therefore, that the Soviet Union shot down a U-2 spy plane piloted by Francis Gary Powers on 1 May 1960.

Oswald Was a Soviet Agent

It was noteworthy that Oswald seemed to live beyond his means while in Japan. He dated a hostess from one of the most expensive nightclubs, whose attentions for one night would cost a month's pay. How could he afford such a woman? The answer becomes obvious, says Pacepa, if we realize that Oswald had "Soviet spy" writ-

ten all over him. When his work in Japan was finished, Oswald didn't want to be in the Marine Corps any longer. What he wanted was to live in the worker's paradise—the Union of Soviet Socialist Republics. So Lee Harvey Oswald defected to the Soviet Union in October 1959. After helping the Soviets to track and shoot down the U-2 spy plane, Oswald was trained by the KGB as an assassin and returned to the United States.

According to Pacepa, it was standard practice for an agent like Oswald to carry a fake diary (created by disinformation specialists) as part of his "legend." Oswald had such a diary, an obvious fabrication with British spellings and expressions (due to the fact that Russian special services were not trained in American English until 1964). Another standard practice was to pair recruited American agents with wives from Soviet bloc countries, so that the wives could keep watch on them. As it happens, Oswald returned to the United States with a Russian wife.

Khrushchev Hated Kennedy

As for Pacepa's sensational assertion about [Soviet premier Nikita] Khrushchev dispatching Oswald to kill Kennedy, the following points are offered by the former Soviet bloc insider: First, Pacepa's superiors in Romanian intelligence thought that Khrushchev intended to kill JFK. What was Khrushchev's motive? First there was the Bay of Pigs invasion of Cuba, which earned Kennedy the KGB codename "Pig." Hoping for a weak liberal in the White House, Khrushchev was seriously disappointed. Instead of a willing dupe, Kennedy proved to be a strong anti-Communist. Khrushchev angrily told his colleagues that Kennedy was an "arrogant millionaire" and a "warmongering fanatic manipulated by the CIA."

Bolstered by the CIA's failed Bay of Pigs invasion, Khrushchev decided to force the Americans to give up West Berlin. "If Kennedy wanted war," explained Pacepa,

Photo on previous page: Lee Harvey Oswald married Marina Prusakova in Minsk in the Soviet Union. After his 1959 defection to the USSR, Oswald asked that his U.S. citizenship "be revoked." **(Fotoresearch/Getty Images.)**

"that was his problem—the Soviet Union would have no choice but to accept his challenge." Kennedy called Khrushchev's bluff, however. "We cannot and will not permit the Communists to drive us out of Berlin, either gradually or by force," said Kennedy. According to Pacepa, Romanian intelligence found that Kennedy had ordered "contingency plans for using nuclear weapons against the Soviet Union" should the crisis escalate.

Khrushchev knew only too well that he had few if any ways to reach the United States with Soviet nuclear weapons. Most Soviet missiles weren't able to fly as far as the United States in those days. What was the Kremlin's solution? Khrushchev decided to secretly deploy more than 50,000 Soviet troops to Cuba along with nuclear-tipped missiles that could threaten Washington and New York—allowing Khrushchev to resume his push against West Berlin. Once again, Kennedy opposed the Soviet leader with a blockade of Cuba. As a result, Khrushchev removed the missiles from Cuba. But Khrushchev would not forgive Kennedy. According to Pacepa, the leader of Communist Romania returned from a trip to Moscow and said, "The lunatic [Khrushchev] is so furious at Kennedy that he's ready to tear him limb from limb with his bare teeth!"

> Khrushchev wanted to liquidate President Kennedy. There is no doubt he had a motive.

In terms of Khrushchev's character, and his readiness to order a hit on the American president, Pacepa wrote: "Today people remember Khrushchev as a down-to-earth peasant who corrected the evils of [Joseph] Stalin. But he was not. The Khrushchev I knew was a compulsive political chatterbox who had no objective appreciation of facts, and who had gotten a taste for the simple criminal solution because of his close association with Stalin's mass killings."

The Soviets Had Arranged Assassinations Before

It is well known that Stalin and Khrushchev both dispatched assassins to the West. In the late 1930s Stalin called for the head of his former colleague, Leon Trotsky. As history records, Ramón Mercader fatally stabbed Trotsky with an ice pick in Mexico. Not only did Stalin reward the assassin's mother with the Order of Lenin, but in 1961 Khrushchev rewarded Mercader with the highest decoration the Kremlin could offer, Hero of the Soviet Union.

As for Khrushchev's assassination exploits, they were exposed in the case of Bogdan Stashinsky, who confessed to a West German court that he had assassinated two "enemies of the Soviet Union" on Khrushchev's orders. There is also the case of Nikolai Khokhlov, who defected to the West in the midst of an assassination mission. According to Pacepa, Khrushchev wanted to liquidate President Kennedy. There is no doubt he had a motive. In Oswald he found the means.

> After Kennedy's death, this idea [that the CIA killed him] was propagated on orders from Moscow to divert attention away from the Kremlin.

It is, of course, a fact that many Americans believe the CIA assassinated President Kennedy. After Kennedy's death, this idea was propagated on orders from Moscow to divert attention away from the Kremlin. This propaganda effort is described by Pacepa, and has been documented in the work of former KGB archive specialist Vasili Mitrokhin.

Rather than accepting the KGB disinformation line about the Kennedy assassination, Americans should read Pacepa's book and judge for themselves.

VIEWPOINT 7

The Kennedy Assassination Will Change from a Political Issue to a Historical Curiosity

Peter Knight

In the following viewpoint, a British scholar argues that despite the still-strong interest in the Kennedy assassination, it will fade from a live political issue to a historical curiosity, just as the assassination of Abraham Lincoln did. Professional historians and investigators have been trumped by amateurs, he says. The movie *JFK* was probably the high-water mark for interest in conspiracy theories and, while it is unlikely that any proof will appear, they will continue to be believed. Moreover, the death of JFK is no longer the most traumatic event remembered by living Americans; the terrorist attacks of September 11, 2001,

---

SOURCE. Peter Knight, *The Kennedy Assassination*. Edinburgh University Press, 2007. www.euppublishing.com.

have overshadowed it. Amateur theorists are now alleging a conspiracy in the case of 9/11, which in time may cause public opinion to diverge from the official version of what happened. Peter Knight is a senior lecturer in American studies at the University of Manchester in England.

Oliver Stone's *JFK* probably represents the high-water mark for public interest in a conspiracy theory of the Kennedy assassination. It was an enormously successful and influential film, reinvigorating debates about the assassination, with a populist groundswell of concern prompting Congress to pass the President John F. Kennedy Assassination Records Collection Act in 1992. At one point in the year leading up to the thirtieth anniversary of the event, half the books on the *New York Times* best-seller list were about the assassination.

Although there has been a steady flow of books, television documentaries and the usual sensational revelations, it is unlikely that the Kennedy assassination will ever again command the national interest in quite the same way as it did after the Stone film, or in the agitation for a Congressional re-opening of the inquiry in the mid-1970s, or in the immediate aftermath of the event in 1963. It is remarkable how the event continues to function as a lightening rod for the charged debates about the meaning of the 1960s, yet ultimately it is almost certainly destined to go the way of other historical controversies such as Pearl Harbor and the Lincoln assassination. Both of the latter, for example, are surrounded by a thriving subculture of conspiracy theory and revisionist history, along with the usual historical tourism that such controversies generate, but neither can be said to have any real impact on present-day politics. The Kennedy assassination will in all likelihood slowly fade from being a live political issue to becoming a historical curiosity. It

A President Who Could Inspire

After the lethargies of the Eisenhower years, John Kennedy seemed to challenge people in all walks to "do better"—one of his favorite phrases—as in his inaugural address [when] he had urged Americans to ask "what you can do for your country." In 1961 and thereafter, there was an avalanche of response—in the Peace Corps, elsewhere in the federal service, in voluntary and private enterprises—almost as if Americans were glad to resume their natural energies. Even of difficult goals, those not to be finished in 1,000 days "nor even perhaps in our lifetime on this planet," he urged, "let us begin."

A president who could lead and inspire: We never cease to need them, but we have had, and no doubt will have, too few.

So even aside from Kennedy's concrete achievements in the Cuban missile crisis, in civil rights and in disarmament, though his time in office lasted only a few years and his [private] conduct seems in retrospect to have been less than pristine, no ordinary president rode in that last motorcade, on that sunlit day, through those cheering crowds in Dallas, to the shattering moment in front of the School Book Depository. For all I know or care, John Kennedy may have played such tricks before high heaven as make the angels weep, but for a while he lifted his people and, as he had promised, got his country moving again.

Therefore, neither Republicans nor Democrats, liberals nor conservatives, nor any of the rest of us should ask for whom the bell tolled on November 22, 1963.

SOURCE. *Tom Wicker, Introduction to* Four Days in November. *Robert B. Semple Jr., ed., St. Martin's, 2003, pp. 19–20.*

is improbable that there will be a definitive death-bed confession or the discovery of a case-breaking smoking gun that will finally prove the existence of a conspiracy, not least because there have already been so many confessions and revelations billed as such. Nor is it likely that the lone gunman version will suddenly win the day, as conspiracy theories are too deeply entrenched in the public consciousness to be easily forgotten.

The Victory of Amateur Theorists Over Authorities

Over the four decades since Kennedy's violent death in Dealey Plaza, the event has been interpreted and represented in ever-widening contexts, but several themes have become constant. The iconic phrases and images that sum up the event—the grassy knoll, the sniper's lair, the magic bullet, the head-snap, Jackie scrambling over the back of the limousine—have become a kind of verbal and visual shorthand for a loss of faith in the authorities and the official version of events, and a more general sense of nostalgic grief for the demise of the promise of youth and idealism supposedly embodied by Kennedy. In short, the flashbulb memories of the assassination (which . . . have largely been retrospectively posited in a form of collective false memory syndrome) provide an instant iconography of the 1960s in general and the loss of an exceptionalist sense of American national destiny in particular.

> The iconic phrases and images that sum up the event . . . have become a kind of verbal and visual shorthand for a loss of faith in the authorities and the official version of events.

If the Kennedy assassination has been the site of a struggle over the authority to retell national history, who has won the day? Perhaps it is still too early to tell, but from the current vantage point it seems—if opinion polls are accurate—that the eyewitness journalists, professional historians and government investigators have all been trumped by a rag-tag bunch of amateur conspiracy researchers, novelists and film makers. Although by now few people are well versed in the specifics of the various conflicting conspiracy theories, three quarters of Americans claim to believe that there was some form of conspiracy involved in the Kennedy assassination, and that it was linked to the other political assassinations of the 1960s. For some commentators this has been hailed as a triumph of grassroots democratic activism, but if it turns out (as I tend to suspect) that Oswald after all acted alone, then this victory of the people vs. the authorities might ultimately seem a hollow one. Whatever the final truth of the case, important lessons have been learned—albeit slowly and painfully—about the damage that an institutionalised practice of government secrecy has on democratic politics.

> Three quarters of Americans claim to believe that there was some form of conspiracy involved in the Kennedy assassination.

The Rise of Conspiracy Theories About 9/11

With the terrorist attacks of 11 September 2001, the meaning of the Kennedy assassination has shifted once again. No longer is the death of JFK the most significant traumatic event for living Americans, not least because two-thirds of Americans alive today were born after 22 November 1963. If the news networks learned on the job during the Kennedy assassination how to cover a breaking story of major importance, then they had perfected the art by the time of the terrorist attacks—although 9/11, like 11/22, also seemed to defy comprehension or belief at first. Like the Kennedy assassination, the strikes on the World Trade Center and the Pentagon have been interpreted in the exaggerated, exceptionalist language of a watershed event that came out of the blue.

As the "Tribute in Light" suggests, the 9/11 attacks have overshadowed the Kennedy assassination in the collective memory of the United States. **(Rick Gershon/ Getty Images.)**

But one of the most interesting developments has been the emergence—slow at first, but now spreading rapidly both within the USA and abroad—of a conspiracist interpretation of 9/11. Although at first sight it seems that everything about the 9/11 attacks was painfully visible and documented from the outset in live television coverage, the case has already become mired in arcane debates that interpret the existing imagery in surprising ways. As with the Kennedy assassination, at first sceptics merely suggested that there were anomalies in the 9/11 Commission Report, another monumental effort of government investigation. But others in the so-called 9/11 Truth Movement have increasingly been focused on the idea that the [George W.] Bush administration was either involved in a cover-up, or even that there was a cabal within the government and the intelligence agencies that was actively involved in planning the attacks. As with the turn to all-encompassing conspiracy theories of political assassinations in the late 1960s and early 1970s, 9/11 is now often inserted by conspiracy researchers into a long sequence of official lies and double-dealing, in some versions leading back to the Kennedy assassination and beyond, as part of a massive postwar conspiracy that secretly controls the reins of power in the Western world. Some well-known Kennedy assassination researchers such as Jim Marrs are now writing books alleging massive conspiracies in the case of 9/11, and some of the grassroots 9/11 conspiracy research organisations acknowledge their debt to JFK conspiracy buffs for their pioneering work in using the Freedom of Information Act to obtain official documents, and for showing them how to connect the dots of a vast conspiracy theory. It is entirely possible that in time 9/11 will become like the Kennedy assassination, a major event in which the path of public opinion slowly diverges from the official version, with representations of the event becoming a battleground for competing visions of American history.

VIEWPOINT 8

Psychological Factors Will Continue to Prevent Resolution of the Kennedy Case

Karen Patterson

Forty years after the assassination of President John F. Kennedy in Dallas, Texas, the *Dallas Morning News* published the following article about why the event made such a deep impression on Americans and why the wound may never heal. It marked a major change in attitude, historians say. After the tragedy, people who had formerly trusted the federal government ceased to do so. The widespread grief was so deep that nearly half of those surveyed reported physical symptoms. The public has continued to be fascinated by conspiracy theories because there is no way to resolve the unanswered questions. Psychologists say that, when reviewing evidence supporting different theories, even

---

people who hadn't been born at the time believe that it supports whatever belief they already held. Furthermore, people will always wonder what might have happened if Kennedy had lived. Karen Patterson is a staff writer for the *Dallas Morning News*.

Four decades later, time hasn't healed this wound.

The killing of John F. Kennedy left a deep and stunning gash in the national psyche. Who President Kennedy was, what he represented, and the optimism of his era made his slaying psychologically personal to much of the nation. Beneath that scar, mistrust and disillusionment still fester—products of a profound national grief, the mystery surrounding the murder, and nagging notions of what might have been.

The fatal shots in Dallas on November 22, 1963, heralded a new era in American attitudes. The public's confidence was shattered.

Few observers expect the mistrust to ever fade, or the wound to ever heal.

"It's a scar because it's an unsolved murder, let's face it," says communication professor Barbie Zelizer, of the University of Pennsylvania. "The more we look at the Kennedy assassination, the more questions that arise. And we don't like our history that way."

Furthermore, to accept that Kennedy's murder was the act of an insignificant malcontent, some experts say, is to accept that hope may be an illusion, and that modern enlightenment could be just a myth.

"Somehow it is more satisfying to believe that a president died as the victim of a cause rather than at the hands of a deranged gunman," writes Thomas Reed Turner, a scholar of the Abraham Lincoln assassination.

The fatal shots in Dallas on November 22, 1963, heralded a new era in American attitudes. The public's confidence was shattered. People who trusted the federal government most of the time, or almost always, fell from a peak of 76 percent soon after the killing to a low of 21 percent three decades later, data from the National Election Studies show.

"There's such a gulf in history between the day before and the day after his assassination," says historian Howard Jones of the University of Alabama. "It's as if we passed through a hundred years in a day."

Man and Myth

Kennedy's ability to captivate many Americans—and many more after his death—is one reason it's so hard to let go of the questions surrounding his murder.

The president cultivated an image of youth and vigor, of ideas and inspiration, of faith and service. He was rich and handsome, and seemed to be such a family man. His untimely death didn't allow the public to see him grow old and bitter, historians have noted, or to see the political sausage-making necessary to turn many of his ideas into action.

And just as a eulogy transcends the warts of the deceased, a mourning nation quickly elevated the dead president to astronomical popularity. Only three years before, voters had favored him by the narrowest of margins.

"When Kennedy was shot, for four days there was nothing on television but stuff about Kennedy, all complimentary," explains political scientist Sheldon Appleton of Oakland University in Rochester, Michigan. Subsequent surveys of those who had voted in 1960 showed so many people selecting Kennedy that, if everyone were remembering correctly, he would have won by a landslide, Dr. Appleton says.

Mythologizing is not unique to the Kennedy assassination, adds Dr. Appleton. Lincoln, Washington and Truman, among others, have all been nearly deified since their deaths.

And right after Martin Luther King Jr. won the Nobel Peace Prize, he received higher negative ratings from the public than did Richard Nixon the week he quit his presidency in disgrace, Dr. Appleton says. "People forget that a lot of people did not like Martin Luther King. Now he's an icon."

A Traumatized Nation

For the millions who mourned Kennedy, the grief and disbelief that followed his killing left a mark that is indelible to this day. Many likened the event to the death of a family member.

Vast majorities of Americans pitied Kennedy's family, research from the time shows. They mourned his loss at the height of his power. They felt shame that such a thing happened in America.

The assassination hurt physically, too, according to an examination of Americans' symptoms just afterward. Roughly half the people surveyed nationally reported crying, feeling dazed and numb, or having trouble sleeping. Other symptoms included loss of appetite, nervousness, dizziness, clammy hands, racing hearts, headaches and upset stomachs.

> While unique in the modern era, Kennedy was not the first president to be so mourned—Lincoln, too, was remembered as kin.

The shock of the event was much like that surrounding the terrorist attacks of September 11, 2001, says Bradley Greenberg, co-editor of a 1965 book examining the assassination and its social fallout. "In both cases, the kind of sequence people went through is that grief period that comes with the death of a loved one," says Dr. Greenberg, who edited a similar collection on public and media responses to 9/11.

A 1966 article explored the phenomenon of group grief after the assassination, noting that rarely do groups identify as closely with an individual as another individual does. "In the case of President Kennedy, however," the *Nursing Forum* article said, "the identification of the people with the lost person was so strong that the grief of the group had the intensity characteristic for individual grief."

While unique in the modern era, Kennedy was not the first president to be so mourned—Lincoln, too, was remembered as kin, says Dr. Turner, whose book *Beware the People Weeping* explores public opinion after the Lincoln assassination. "Soldiers saw him as 'Father Lincoln,'" Dr. Turner says. And the public spoke of Lincoln's slaying "as being a family kind of thing—'our father is gone.'"

What If?

The death of anyone before his time inevitably leaves survivors considering what might have happened, had the person lived.

The loss of Lincoln, after the hard-won Civil War, was marked by a sense of unfulfilled destiny, says Dr. Turner. "Lincoln got the American people to the Promised Land," people thought, "but God didn't allow him to cross over and see the fruits of this victory."

> Thoughts of what Kennedy might have accomplished have dogged his followers for decades.

Similarly, thoughts of what Kennedy might have accomplished have dogged his followers for decades. In particular, the Kennedy killing touches on another very sore spot on the national psyche: the war in Vietnam.

Perhaps, says Dr. Jones, the 58,000 American deaths—and thousands more in Southeast Asia—might have been avoided had Kennedy lived.

The great, unspoken truth in the 1963 White House, Dr. Jones learned, was that a U.S. war in Vietnam could not be won. So the president, Dr. Jones says, was firm in resisting pressure to beef up military aid to South Vietnam. "He would grant military advice, economic aid, but he was not going to take over the war—it was their war," says Dr. Jones, whose new book *Death of a Generation* discusses how Kennedy planned to withdraw from Vietnam.

Kennedy planned first to withdraw 1,000 military personnel in late 1963 and then continue through 1965 to prune their ranks to 1961 levels, says Dr. Jones.

That plan was derailed by the unfolding of religious and political events in South Vietnam—first, a violent clash between Buddhists and the Catholic regime of Ngo Dinh Diem, punctuated worldwide by a photo of a monk setting himself afire in downtown Saigon. Then Diem, who was to be ousted with Kennedy's tacit endorsement, was killed.

Expecting to face staunch conservative Barry Goldwater in the 1964 election and fearing he'd be branded soft on communism, the president decided to wait until after his re-election to withdraw from Vietnam, Dr. Jones says.

Before that could happen, Kennedy was killed.

The Toppling of Kings

A mere week after Kennedy's assassination, Gallup polling found that only 29 percent of Americans thought that Lee Harvey Oswald acted alone.

Accepting that lone killers slew presidents James Garfield in 1881 and William McKinley in 1901 was much easier, says Dr. Turner. For one thing, the trauma over their deaths wasn't as great. The public hardly knew Garfield, who was shot after just four months in office. McKinley had presided over the popular Spanish-American War, but didn't achieve the monumental status Lincoln did. And both assassins seemed overtly disturbed: Garfield's killer believed God told him to do it; McKinley's appeared paranoid and claimed to be an anarchist.

Lincoln's killing has not been put to rest as easily. Amateur historians took up the case for more than a century, Dr. Turner says, before he and other pros weighed in.

The Lincoln assassination in fact was an effort of a band of conspirators, led by John Wilkes Booth, Dr. Turner notes. But whether there was a wider conspiracy—that is, whether the Confederate secret service induced Booth to try to kidnap Lincoln—has been debated for about two decades. "The Lincoln assassination is still wide open," he says.

In any case, it's just human nature to first think "conspiracy" when the course of a nation is so swiftly changed, suggests Dr. Turner, a history professor at Bridgewater State College in Massachusetts.

"If you look back at antiquity, and even some myths in antiquity, and you get a great king, a great figure, and

As with Kennedy, unanswered questions surrounding the assassination of President Abraham Lincoln—immortalized here at the Lincoln Memorial—keep Americans intrigued about his life. **(AP Images.)**

he is slain by somebody who doesn't appear to be as great a figure, even in antiquity people couldn't accept that," says Dr. Turner citing an argument by historian Lloyd Lewis. "It doesn't satisfy people. And that's why I don't think you'll ever close the [Kennedy] case, really."

Reporting the Story

It's also hard to accept something that had no authoritative witnesses, says Dr. Zelizer, a professor at the University of Pennsylvania's Annenberg School for Communication. The media, although ever present in the wake of the assassination, didn't actually *see* what happened, she notes.

Reporters were in the president's motorcade but were a few vehicles back from Kennedy, says Dr. Zelizer, author of *Covering the Body*, a book describing how the media shaped beliefs about the assassination. "So you have people who were eyewitnesses at the side of the road seeing things that the journalists didn't."

Then Oswald was captured. Jack Ruby shot him. The funeral began. Events came faster than reporters could grasp them, Dr. Zelizer says.

Understandably, Dr. Zelizer says, journalists couldn't process all the implications amid the chaos. "The circumstances, however, changed over the years that followed, and their stories did not."

For the most part, she says, journalists stuck to their original story, of a lone assassin, leaving it to independent assassination investigators to explore other possibilities. But, lacking the support and cachet of major media outlets, the credibility of those investigators was hobbled. "Journalists could look at them and say, these guys are crackpots, and not attend to what they were bringing up," Dr. Zelizer says.

She thinks the time has passed when one piece of evidence could be found that would put the Kennedy controversy to rest. "But there were moments when evidence was lost," she laments. "Had there been a more vigilant public sphere, including politicians, including journalists, one might be able to say we might have known things differently."

Witness to History

Meanwhile, over the past forty years, the public has grown more and more accustomed to itself witnessing—via the media—notorious events, notes Dr. Greenberg.

Up-close images were distributed of Robert Kennedy's 1968 assassination, for instance, and the 1981 attempt on Ronald Reagan's life. "Each of those was increasingly available to us to examine," says Dr. Greenberg, a professor of communication and telecommunication at Michigan State University. "We didn't see Oswald pull the trigger."

And nothing has paralleled the public's witnessing of the 2001 terrorist attacks.

"We shared 9/11 in its original moment," Dr. Greenberg says. "Time and again, we saw it."

Who Can Know?

Sheer fascination with conspiracy also appears to fuel the continuing Kennedy flame.

Dr. Appleton has noted the vast number of Web pages devoted to conspiracies—on one search engine, counted before 9/11, there were nearly 350,000.

The Americans who are most likely to embrace conspiracy theories are those with lower education levels, and those who feel alienated from government and political activity, says Dr. Appleton.

His work has also suggested that people with a low tolerance for ambiguity are more likely to be convinced of conspiracies at work. And conspiracy abets conspiracy: People who believe in one are more likely to believe in others.

But all of that doesn't mean Kennedy wasn't the victim of some conspiracy, he says.

"The thing that strikes me is not that people are wrong, but we probably could count on our fingers the number of people who really know, if there are any, whether there was a conspiracy or not," says Dr. Appleton, who researches the nature of assassination and conspiracy beliefs. "How many people could know? Yet so many people seem to be so sure . . . and with such emotion, and such force.

"Those things tell me that the origins of those beliefs lie less in the factual realm than in the emotional realm."

Even Nellie Connally, the Texas first lady who was in the car when Kennedy was shot, says she doesn't know what really happened. The assassination has thus become a kind of Rorschach blot—an ambiguous situation onto which people passionately project their own beliefs, Dr. Appleton says.

Diehard assassination buffs remind him of a line from *The King and I*: "They fight to prove that what they do not know is so."

The Next Generation

Psychological processes even today, and even among those who hadn't yet been born in 1963, appear to make any resolution of the Kennedy tragedy impossible.

For instance, a 1995 study, by social psychologist John McHoskey, demonstrated that people bring their own baggage to the evaluation of the lone assassin vs. conspiracy controversy. The study asked 253 college students, all born after Kennedy was killed, to consider summaries of evidence supporting each theory. Predictably, people on both sides of the debate perceived the same evidence as supporting whichever belief they already held, a process known as biased assimilation.

A wide body of literature demonstrates this process in a number of situations, says Dr. McHoskey, of Eastern Michigan University. "People have a need to feel that they're kind of competent and that they understand the world, that they're smart," he explains. "And one of the ways is that they come up with ideas about how the world is, and they keep convincing themselves that they're right."

Given such tendencies, Dr. McHoskey says, the Kennedy debate is utterly unresolvable. "There's no evidence that could ever materialize that could convince us," he says.

At the same time, the generations newest to the debate have come of age in an era where doubt and disbelief often eclipse trust and faith. Compare this with the naiveté of 1963.

"You're looking at a period in which the bitterness over Vietnam had not hit, the bitterness over Watergate had not hit, the [government] credibility gap had not hit," Dr. Jones says. "You're looking at a time when if the president said something, you believed it. . . .

"Afterward, people questioned everything."

CHAPTER 3

Personal Narratives

VIEWPOINT 1

Seeing the Reaction to Kennedy's Assassination in Paris

Barbara Bottner

Barbara Bottner was an American college student spending her junior year in Paris to study painting. She was celebrating a friend's birthday with a movie and dinner when the news of President Kennedy's assassination arrived. At first it was just a rumor, but when they came out of the movie they learned it was true and that the French people, who loved Kennedy, were gathering in the streets. Other patrons in the restaurant overheard her group speaking English and bombarded them with questions, thinking they must have known more than was being said on the radio. But they had no further information; like the French, they were stunned. Barbara Bottner worked as a set designer, an actress, and a substitute teacher before becoming an award-winning author of children's books. She has also written for television.

Photo on opposite page: How Jacqueline Kennedy endured the aftermath of the assassination became, for many Americans, a barometer of overall U.S. well-being. **(George Silk/Time Life Pictures/Getty Images.)**

SOURCE. Barbara Bottner, "JFK" in *We'll Never Be Young Again: Remembering the Last Days of John F. Kennedy*, Charles Fries and Irv Wilson, eds. Beverly Hills, CA: Tallfellow Press, 2003.

Paris, France, November 22, 1963. I was at the Ecole Des Beaux Arts, studying painting for my junior year abroad.

It was Matthew Robbins' birthday. Susan Dalsimer, Walter Murch and I were going to celebrate him turning 20. We were in Paris, driving around on motorcycles, so we didn't need a lot to make us happy. A movie, Truffaut's *Quatre Cing Coups*, then a cheap dinner somewhere on the Left Bank.

As we went into the cinema, we heard a rumor to the effect that President Kennedy had been wounded. We were worried, but the reports were unreliable, mostly rumor. The French love gossip. The information that was floating around wasn't clear. What was not told in the United States for hours was still pretty vague in our time zone, five hours later. Whatever worries we had abated as the movie began. (Matthew and Walter were both to become screenwriters and directors; Walter would subsequently win three Academy Awards. Susan was to become a VP at Warners and publisher of Miramax Books. Movies, well, they were movies, and we were hearing them in a second language. That took up most of our concentration.)

> "There was a sort of pandemonium in the streets. . . . Kennedy was beloved in France."

There was a sort of pandemonium in the streets when we emerged. Kennedy was beloved in France. Now it was ten o'clock [in the evening] in France, 5:00 P.M. in the United States. The story was becoming clearer. We began to understand that he was shot and mortally wounded. But, then, we heard "*non, non*" he was not dead, merely in the hospital. He was going to recover. Then, "*non, non,*" he was, in fact, dead. Definitely dead.

The more we tried to understand that he might be dead, the more stupefied we became.

The French Asked Questions

We were hungry and in shock. We went to the famous [café] Les Deaux Maggots. Normally, we would not have paid the price for dinner there, but that night, budgets mattered not.

Over French bread, we attempted to grapple with the events. We tried to overhear what the French patrons were saying, but as soon as they overheard us speaking English they bombarded us with questions, assuming that by being American, we must have had more information than they did. The French are conspiratorialists. They wanted us to give them theories. Then the history of the politics of Texas, explain the motives, the possible enemies; they wanted a history lesson in American politics. We wanted to know what the radio was saying. We could hardly eat.

Finally, we began to walk down the crowded streets. Everyone was out that night and talking or arguing with each other.

Matthew and I walked ahead of Susan and Walter. We were not at our most vigilant. Some Algerians asked me to look at their map. We felt a brotherhood that night, as people do during catastrophes. I stopped to help them.

Matthew is wiry and hardly intimidating. An Algerian and his friend surrounded me and begin to pull me towards a car as if they were going to kidnap me. There was a fair amount of white slave trade then, and I was young.

Perhaps I would not be living in a lovely street called Rainbow Drive now, if Walter, who is well over six feet, hadn't gleaned what was going on. He strode up behind us and bellowed, "What the hell do you think you are doing?"

The Algerians ran off into the crowded Parisian streets, merging into the stunned population. It was as if evil itself was there in the streets of Paris, too.

VIEWPOINT 2

A Service Officer Experiences the Aftermath of Kennedy's Death in West Berlin

Lucian Heichler

At the time of President Kennedy's assassination, the city of Berlin was isolated deep inside Communist-controlled East Germany and was divided in two by a tall concrete wall. West Berlin consisted of the portions of the city occupied by the United States, Great Britain, and France after World War II, and its people lived in fear of an East German takeover. They were strong admirers of Kennedy—who just a few months before had made a famous speech there expressing American support—and were deeply affected by his death. Lucian Heichler, who was a young U.S. foreign service officer there, describes their reaction in the following narrative. He is now a retired senior U.S. diplomat.

SOURCE. Lucian Heichler, "How Berlin Mourned John F. Kennedy," *American Diplomacy*, May 30, 2002.

In the evening of November 22, 1963, the cultural affairs officer of U.S. Mission Berlin hosted a reception for young Fulbright scholarship students recently returned from their stay in the United States. When I arrived at his home a few minutes before eight, someone had turned on the radio to catch the AFN [American Forces Network] news. We heard the fateful words, "The President has been shot. . . ." Within minutes the announcer confirmed the worst: "The President is dead."

The reception ended immediately; the guests left quickly and quietly. Much the same thing was happening all over the city, but I did not know that yet. I learned only later that everywhere in West Berlin stage, film and concert performances ended abruptly, bars and restaurants closed, private dinners and parties broke up. Trained to respond like a homing pigeon, I headed straight for my office in the U.S. mission on Clay-Allee. A young Foreign Service officer assigned to the mission's political section, I held the special and unusual position of liaison officer to the West Berlin city government, then headed by Governing Mayor Willy Brandt. Without waiting for a summons, a number of the military and Foreign Service officers on the staff of the U.S. Commander Berlin, the Berlin Brigade, and the U.S. mission [State Department] gathered at U.S. headquarters for what turned into an all-night vigil and working session in the "bunker," the rarely used emergency operations center.

Making Arrangements

Almost eagerly we began to attend to mundane, practical matters, partly because it was necessary, partly because it helped us to deal with our own emotions. Once persuaded that there was no international crisis, no need to move to a higher stage of military alert, we became absorbed in questions of protocol—almost like a family suffering a sudden death: What needed to be done? None of us knew the procedures to be followed when a president dies in office. Manuals were consulted, cables were fired off to Washington requesting instructions.

We arranged to buy a number of so-called "condolence books" from Berlin stationery stores, books which would be placed in various public locations around the American Sector of Berlin and opened to people who might want to pay their respects by signing their names. No one dreamed that in the days which followed more than a quarter of a million people would stand patiently in block-long queues, waiting to sign these books. Our military colleagues searched frantically for what army protocol required under these circumstances and came up with a number of proposals, including a special review ceremony to mourn and honor the slain commander-in-chief. This review would be held on the parade grounds of Andrews Barracks, with German and Allied dignitaries invited.

As the students marched, thousands of other people joined the procession so that by midnight about 75,000 people stood in Rudolf-Wilde-Platz.

By coincidence, the student councils of West Berlin's two universities had met in joint session that evening. On learning the tragic news, they instantly adjourned and organized a torch-light procession of students to march to the Rathaus, West Berlin's provisional city hall in the Borough of Schöneberg. As the students marched, thousands of other people joined the procession so that by midnight about 75,000 people stood in Rudolf-Wilde-Platz in front of the Rathaus, waiting for their mayor to say some words of comfort and reassurance to them.

Only that afternoon Willy Brandt had returned from an exhausting two-week swing around West Africa. He had gone to bed and was asleep, his wife Ruth told us when we phoned his residence. Frantically, we insisted that he must be awakened to hear the terrible news. Thus it was that at one o'clock in the morning on November 23 Brandt appeared before the huge crowd assembled in front of city hall and announced to them that he personally would fly to Washington to represent Berlin at the funeral two days hence of the American president. At the hour of the funeral his deputy, Mayor Heinrich Albertz, would preside over a commemorative rally to be held in front of city hall—the same spot where Kennedy had addressed jubilant Berliners only a few months earlier.

A Military Review

The American military review to honor the memory of the fallen commander in chief was deeply moving. Never before or since have I witnessed the quiet, measured step—more of a loping stride than a march step—of infantry marching to the beat of muffled drums. The ceremony was concluded with the playing of "Taps," rendered exceptionally moving by an echo effect achieved by two buglers posted at opposite ends of the parade ground, echoing the haunting melody back and forth between them. Brandt was so taken with this that he turned to me to ask that I make exactly the same arrangements for the Rathaus memorial service. I transmitted the Mayor's request; accordingly, Berlin Brigade sent the two buglers downtown. One stood on the Rathaus roof, the other atop an office building across the square. The effect was every bit as beautiful as it had been at Andrews Barracks.

> Gradually it began to dawn on us what John F. Kennedy had really meant to these people, and especially to the youth of Germany and the world, how to them he had been a symbol of hope.

For Monday, the day of the funeral in Washington, U.S. military protocol prescribed that guns should be fired every minute on the minute, all through the long day, until evening. For this purpose Berlin Brigade drew up six 105-mm howitzers in the courtyard of American Headquarters, deploying three of the self-propelled guns on each side of the central flagpole. These guns fired in rotation, one every minute, like rhythmic, rolling thunder, all the day long, providing a somber background and punctuation to our work in the building.

About 4:30 in the afternoon that day a bugler and a platoon of infantry came marching up to the flagpole to conduct a simple retreat ceremony. Along with one or two other people still in the building I went downstairs to attend. I watched as the flag was slowly lowered; I listened to the bugler playing "Taps" against the background of the guns booming away with their sullen, somber regularity—and at that moment something snapped; I was finally overcome by emotion and gave way to tears.

Condolences from Berliners

That weekend, and in the days and weeks to follow, we Americans in Berlin received condolence calls and notes not only from many Berlin friends and neighbors but also, most movingly, from many total strangers. Waitresses we had hired for one dinner or reception called or wrote to express their sorrow and sympathy. Gradually it began to dawn on us what John F. Kennedy had really meant to these people, and especially to the youth of Germany and the world, how to them he had been a symbol of hope—one leader, at last, in whom they dared to place their confidence and their faith.

The hour of the Trauerfeier—literally the "festival of mourning"—at city hall drew nigh. Once again, as on that beautiful, sunny day in June, hundreds of thousands of Berliners filled the square in front of the Rathaus. But what a terrible contrast: In place of bright sunshine, cold drizzle in the foggy darkness; instead of cheering, chanting crowds, a sad and largely silent throng of mourners. For the first time since the occupation of Berlin, the city government had asked that an Allied military honor guard be posted there: A platoon of American soldiers stood at attention and presented arms across the front of the Rathaus. Mayor Albertz and other dignitaries delivered their eulogies.

As I sat among the other invited guests in the hastily erected bleachers, I reflected on the stark and terrible contrast between this sad hour and the electrifying moment when John Kennedy had stood here and told the madly cheering crowd, "*Ich bin ein Berliner!*" ["I am a Berliner!"] . . .

A mere five months later, John Kennedy lay dead in the Rotunda of the Capitol in Washington, and none of us were yet able to comprehend the senseless tragedy which had befallen us. How have the myth, the hope, the promise fared in Germany in the years since November 22, 1963?

Inevitably, Kennedy's image has become somewhat tarnished over the years, and Europeans are less aware than knowledgeable Americans that Kennedy's presidency was already beset by increasing difficulties when he was assassinated. Nevertheless, to a remarkable extent the myth of Camelot lives on, especially among the Germans east of the Elbe River, liberated from communist dictatorship only seven years ago [1989]. The Kennedy myth lives on.

VIEWPOINT 3

Walking a Horse in President Kennedy's Funeral Procession

Arthur A. Carlson

Since ancient times there has been a tradition of walking a riderless horse in the funeral processions of high-ranking military officers. As president, John F. Kennedy was the nation's commander-in-chief, so he was given a military funeral and buried in Arlington National Cemetery. The horse Black Jack often took part in funerals at the cemetery, but for Kennedy's there were several long processions through Washington, DC, too, during which he became excited and hard to control. Arthur A. Carlson, his regular handler, was a nineteen-year-old soldier at the time. In the following narrative he describes what happened during the funeral.

SOURCE. Arthur A. Carlson, "Personal Memoirs of the State Funeral of President John F. Kennedy, November 22–25, 1963," edited by Kenneth S. Pond, Thomas F. Reid, Edward M. Gripkey, and James W. McElroy, 2008. Thomas © Thomas F. Reid. Reproduced by permission.

When President Kennedy was assassinated, I was in an off-post laundromat. I had been Charge of Quarters (CQ) in the stable the night before and had the day off and was doing my laundry. When I was walking back to our barracks, I passed some people clustered around a car, listening to the radio. That is when I learned of the assassination. I was stunned.

At the time I was a 19-year-old Private First Class in The Old Guard at Fort Myer, Virginia, and had been walking the caparisoned horse (usually Black Jack, sometimes Shorty) in funerals in Arlington National Cemetery (ANC) for about nine months. The caparisoned horse in a military funeral procession is an ancient tradition, symbolizing a fallen leader who will ride no more. A caparison is "an ornamental covering for a horse or for its saddle or harness." A caparisoned horse with walker will follow a caisson in a funeral at ANC if the deceased was an Army or Marine Corps colonel or above, or had ever served in a mounted outfit. The horse's tack consists of bridle, saddle and blanket, boots and saber. The boots are turned backward in the stirrups to symbolize the fallen leader looking back over his past life.

Black Jack

I led the caparisoned horse throughout the State Funeral for President John F. Kennedy in November 1963. Black Jack (named for General "Black Jack" Pershing) was the last horse with an Army serial number. He had come from the Remount Station at Fort Reno and had 2CV-56 branded on the left side of his neck, and US branded on his left flank. He had very small hooves, and no one was allowed to ride him.

Chief Warrant Officer John McKinney, the leader of the Caisson Platoon, picked the White Horse Section for the caisson, and named Black Jack and me for the JFK funeral. My usual replacement would ride Swing with the caisson. Black Jack was taller than Shorty, with an even temperament. Shorty was an evil kicker who did not deal well with loud noises. Last year I got a phone call from the first man who walked Black Jack in funerals. He said that Black Jack was wild when he arrived at Caisson Platoon. It took six months to settle him enough to use him in funerals, and he still would dance a lot. We knew nothing about this.

My first part in the funeral was to follow the caisson as it carried the casket from the White House to the Capitol Building, to lie in state. To reach the White House, Black Jack and I followed the caisson from the stable at Fort Myer, through Arlington National Cemetery, across Memorial Bridge, to the courtyard inside the Treasury Building. We waited there for a time, resting and checking everything again. I think it was then we heard that Lee Harvey Oswald had been killed, and wondered what was happening to our country.

> "All the TV people had talked constantly about Black Jack and the soldier with him. The horse had the public's attention."

Black Jack was calm. It was the proverbial calm before the storm. When told to move out we exited through a narrow street-level tunnel, barely large enough for the horses and caisson. A large steel grate was leaning against a wall inside the tunnel, and the hub of the right rear wheel of the caisson hooked it and started dragging it along the cobblestone paving and the stone wall. The noise inside the tunnel was huge, and Black Jack went wild. He stayed agitated for the next three days, for the entire funeral.

Our usual position was behind the caisson, and facing it. At the White House, instead of standing steady, Black Jack constantly threw his head and danced around me. After about 10 seconds people stopped crowding us and gave us space. We carried the president's body from the White House to the Capitol. Then we moved out and walked back to the stable. When we got there, the few men who had stayed to take care of the other horses said that all the TV people had talked constantly about Black Jack and the soldier with him. The horse had the public's attention.

We took care of the horses and tack, and then watched tapes of the first day on the TV set in the CQ room. It was a chance to critique everything we had done, look for opportunities for improvement. We hoped that Black Jack would settle down before the next part of the funeral.

> "I tried to stand at parade rest holding [Black Jack's] bridle—at least one of us should behave in proper military fashion."

The Funeral Procession

After the president had lain in state, we went back to the Capitol. Black Jack continued to act up. We moved the president's body to Saint Matthew's Cathedral for the final service. I saw Charles DeGaulle and Haile Salassie, men who influenced history, among the mourners, and also Mrs. Kennedy and Prince Philip of England. I have never seen a crowd so still and silent. We heard later that when Prince Philip was designated to represent England, he was told there was no need to hurry—it would take at least 2 weeks to plan and execute such a funeral.

The route was lined with soldiers on both sides standing at parade rest. As the caisson neared they would come to attention. I felt sorry for men having to stand so still for so long. One man who had that duty said that he felt something in his hand behind his back, and a woman whispered, "It's a sugar cube. Put it in your mouth and suck it when you get the chance." From the corner of his eye he saw a female major going to each soldier.

At the cathedral people again decided not to crowd Black Jack and me. I tried to stand at parade rest holding his bridle—at least one of us should behave in proper military fashion. At one point he was pawing the pave-

ment and struck my right shoe. I was afraid some toes might be broken. Later I found that the shoe was ruined, but no bones were broken. The shoe had to be replaced.

Police officers were doing crowd control. Two of them were quietly chatting up a couple of young women, and then their lieutenant came over and spoke to them in a deadly whisper, and they were silent.

After the funeral service, we headed toward Arlington National Cemetery. Black Jack continued to dance and throw his head strongly. I was getting desperately tired, especially my right arm, but knew that if that horse got away from me I would be walking guard around a radar station in Greenland before the week was out.

At one point bagpipes played. I had trouble getting the beat, but once I learned to march with the music it gave me a burst of energy. That is music to fight by. Then the pipes went silent, and the energy burst faded. By Memorial Bridge I was so tired I had to make a choice—good posture or keep step with the drumbeat. I chose keeping in step.

At the gravesite, Black Jack and I would normally move to the front wheel of the caisson opposite the grave, and face the casket as it was carried from caisson to grave. This time we could not do that because the crowd was so thick, and Black Jack was back on home territory and too tired to make room for us.

As we stood behind the caisson the Air Force did a Missing Man flyover, and then Air Force One flew over alone. It was almost over, and I allowed myself to choke up. Then the firing party fired three volleys and Taps was played. The bugler broke on one note of Taps—we assumed he got choked up, too.

We pushed our way through the crowd, and went back through the cemetery to our stable. We took care of our horses and tack, and it was almost over. We got a phone call that Mrs. Kennedy wanted the tack from Black Jack. I put on a fresh uniform and borrowed some shoes,

Photo on previous pages: Nineteen-year-old Arthur Carlson can be seen leading the riderless horse Black Jack below the flying flag, near its staff, as part of Kennedy's November 24, 1963, funeral cortege. **(George F. Mobley/ National Geographic/ Getty Images.)**

and took all of his tack—cleaned but not polished—to the White House and gave it to a colonel.

A cardinal rule of broadcasting is No Dead Air. On-air personalities are required to talk constantly. Nothing so attracts attention as misbehavior, and that is why Black Jack and the man walking him became famous. In a pre-funeral meeting someone brought up that horses are bad to poop in public—very unsightly, and asked if not feeding them for a day would prevent that. Mr. McKinney asked what the result would be if they did not feed the soldiers for a day before the funeral. He was told that the soldiers would probably pass out. "That is what the horses will do, too." End of discussion.

VIEWPOINT 4

Dealing with Kennedy's Assassination as an Eighth-Grade Teacher

Judy Redick, interviewed by Robert Dixon

Judy Redick was an eighth-grade teacher in Springfield, Illinois, at the time President Kennedy was killed. In the following narrative she recalls how her class reacted to the news, the kind of discussions they had in the days that followed, and her own feelings about the event. Unlike many Americans, Ms. Redick was not an admirer of Kennedy and although her first thought was to pray for him, she did not experience personal grief. She points out that just before the assassination his popularity was at its lowest, which was forgotten because of the sympathy people had for him after he was shot.

SOURCE. Robert Dixon, "Interview with Judy Redick," *John F. Kennedy Assassination: Project Memoir*, 1972. John F. Kennedy Assassination Oral History Project. Archives/Special Collections, Norris L. Brookens Library, University of Illinois at Springfield. Reproduced with permission from University of Illinois at Springfield.

Robert Dixon: Judy, what do you remember about the Kennedy assassination?

Judy Redick: Well, at the time, I think it happened right around lunch time. And I can remember even before it came over the PA system. They called and told me that I had a phone call in the office. I went downstairs and my husband was calling to ask me if I knew that President Kennedy had been shot and they didn't know his condition. By the time I got back upstairs then it came over the PA system for the whole school. And the rest of the afternoon was kind of spent waiting and watching, waiting to hear what had actually happened to him.

Right after I got back upstairs they put it over the PA, that he had been shot. The first thing that came to my mind was that the children should pray for him. And after I had told them that I thought before they did anything else that they should put their heads down on their desk and say a prayer that he wasn't seriously hurt and that he would be all right. Being my first year of teaching I also recall that in the public schools they had banned any kind of group prayer, and I thought at the time that I really didn't care if I would be criticized or possibly even lose my job for this. It was just something that I felt that . . . the only thing we could do at the time was say a prayer for him and then go on with our work.

"The only thing we could do at the time was say a prayer for him and then go on with our work."

It was during the lunch hour or shortly after the lunch hour and the children were just in their homeroom for a short period of time and then moved on to their next class. The rest of the afternoon the other students were pretty quiet waiting to hear more news of what had happened or what was coming next. And the school did keep us pretty well informed over the PA for the whole school. When they got another piece of news then they sent it over the PA system so that the whole student body knew what was going on.

Discussions in Class

Did they have any questions?

No, they didn't question too much. I guess more than anything else they couldn't imagine someone doing this and being eighth-grade students [they] hadn't really studied or known of anything like this happening. In eighth-grade social studies you do study American history, but at the time, this happened in November, school starts in September, and when you have to go from when Columbus discovered America to present day history you aren't too far enough along in the presidency or even past the study of the Constitution to have gotten into any part of history where other presidents had been assassinated. So, this was something that for them was new because there hadn't been a president in real recent history, recent history as far as these eighth graders were concerned, that had been assassinated.

> School was called off for the day and everyone stayed home and watched the funeral on television.

There were questions later the next week when we came back to school. Of course this happened on a Friday and I don't believe we had school on Monday. I think school was called off for the day and everyone stayed home and watched the funeral on television. And by the time we came back on Tuesday then, we did take up discussion of it in the history classes as to other presidents who had been assassinated or shot at and the type of people that had done these things and if there had been motives in doing it and the punishments that had been put upon them. And then, of course, living in Illinois one of our own presidents was assassinated, so it was a good review in history. Something very historical that you could study if you want to look at it that way. It seems kind of cruel to talk of it that way but it was present day history and it was a good way to bring in past U.S. history with what had happened in our country the present day.

After you left the school do you remember anything else that you did over the weekend? Other than maybe watch television.

[My husband and I] watched television almost the entire weekend. In fact, we hadn't been married that terribly long when it happened. We were married in June and it happened in November. And I do remember that we had a portable television and just, of course, black and white, and my folks' television broke over the weekend or broke, I guess, from overplay of what had happened during the assassination and all of the events that followed. And I can remember my parents and my younger sister coming out to watch the proceedings on our television. My mother was very interested in all of it and could have watched it over and over again and especially was interested in Jackie and how well she was holding up through the whole affair and how she took care of her children and had them conduct themselves in the way that they did, which didn't mean much to me at the time because I had no children. But I also remember that we watched it an awful lot. I was interested and I watched it a lot but my husband got bored with it. Got tired of watching the same thing over and over again and we did, I think, leave

> "I really don't think that . . . it would have been a Communist plot because in some ways I think of them being smoother operators."

and go to at least two movies over the weekend because he said he just couldn't watch it any more. So we left the house and went to the theater. But other than that we did pretty much watch it the entire time.

Speculation on a Plot

As a mother or as a teacher you think that with presidents being assassinated, and people in high office being shot at like Governor [George] Wallace and so forth, do you still encourage your students to be interested in politics?

Yes, I would because these things don't happen that often and I think even more so now that that did happen to President Kennedy, the secret service is, well, it seems like they almost really double shift them. And you can watch when you see our president now or past presidents or even presidential candidates have secret service agents with them and I think they are pretty well protected. . . .

Getting back to the assassination. At first some newspapers, television commentators thought that maybe a Communist plot was involved or some radical shot the president for some unknown reason. When you heard about it and thought about it did you have any flash judgments about who would do such a thing?

Well, I really don't think that I thought it would have been a Communist plot because in some ways I think of them being smoother operators, plus if they set out to do a job, it's done. And wouldn't, well, I guess you wouldn't say that Oswald missed because he didn't. He was killed but he didn't die instantly, and I think that if they had been involved that it would have been an instant death, and plus I don't think the fellow would have left himself open to be able to be captured and arrested and have to face trial for punishment of the crime. I really at the time just thought it would have to be a very sick person and just kind of, well, I would call him a radical or a person who is just really almost insane at the time to try and attempt something like this.

Oswald really didn't face trial, you know.

No, he didn't.

He was eliminated.

He was eliminated and I suppose a lot of people could wonder, too, if that was all a plot, if it was conspiracy that Ruby would assassinate him and that the police would handle the situation the way they did because you would never find that in present day circumstances if they had a well-known criminal like that now. They move them at odd hours of the night or take them in unmarked cars and things like this. In other words, at a time and in a way that they think that the press will not be around or anyone else will be around to witness the act or that would draw any kind of a crowd that something like this could happen.

And, of course, directly happening because of the way the Dallas police . . . handled the Oswald affair. Did you see that on TV?

No, we didn't. We'd gone to church. We were early risers, I guess, and went to an early church that day and when we got home other friends called us and asked if we had seen it. They hadn't gone to church yet; they were going to go to a later service and called and wanted to know if we had seen it. And we said, no, that we'd just gotten back in the door. And they said, "Well, you wouldn't believe it because the whole thing happened just right before your eyes." You know, just right on television everybody was an eye witness to the entire affair. And of course, we saw a replay of it later on TV but no, we didn't see it when it actually happened. . . .

Kennedy's Popularity

> I was never a Kennedy fan. I think [the Kennedys] were kind of blown all out of proportion to be the great gods or saviors of the world.

You were a friend of Kennedy's or not?

No, no, I wasn't Kennedy's fan, either. In fact, when he was running for election I think his brother Bobby came to school when I was in college and I didn't even go to see him. No, I was never a Kennedy fan. I think they were kind of blown all out of proportion to be the great gods or saviors of the world. I just never thought they were.

When LBJ did become President and a lot of the social legislation that John Kennedy tried to pass and was always bottled up in the Senate finally was passed, do you think it was passed [as] sort of a memorial to Kennedy or because of [President] Johnson's abilities?

It was probably a combination of the two. At the time that Kennedy was assassinated his popularity was at its lowest. People forgot that soon after, though, because anyone feels sympathy for someone that, you know, something like that happens to them. I think that it probably was passed in a measure as a tribute or memorial to him or out of a feeling of sympathy, but on the other hand the other part of it that would have gotten it through would be Johnson's ways of knowing how to get things through the legislature, how to deal with congressmen to get things passed. He was the master craftsman at that and worked at it for many, many years.

Well now Lincoln was, I think, unpopular when he was alive and Kennedy at the time that he was shot was popular. Do you think that in the future Kennedy would be viewed like Lincoln?

> I [don't] think the whole truth has yet been told or if it ever will be told, but then, maybe what they haven't told they don't feel is good for the country to know.

Well, I don't think his popularity has died out yet so. . . . Boy, that's hard to say because I don't think there is anything in Kennedy's program that would stand out as much as the Civil War when Lincoln was president and the Emancipation Proclamation. Those were two very, very big events. I just can't recall anything right off hand from Kennedy's administration that would make such a mark in history as the Civil War or the Emancipation Proclamation.

The Warren Commission

What did you think of the chief justice of the Supreme Court being appointed to head the committee that investigated the assassination?

I guess at the time, I don't know if I really thought too much about it either way. They should have been as fair a group as any to take it before. These men worked with cases all the time which had heavy biases to each side and they supposedly give an unbiased opinion, so I'm sure that the Supreme Court was as good a place to take something like this to as any. I don't know that I was completely satisfied with the Warren Report, I [don't] think the whole truth has yet been told or if it ever will be told, but then, maybe what they haven't told they don't feel is good for the country to know.

Do you believe what they said about Oswald?

Views on the Kennedy assassination may be as numerous as views on the president himself. (AP Images.)

That he worked by himself?

By himself.

Yes, I don't think he was in with another group. I really think he worked by himself. I don't know about the Jack Ruby business of killing Oswald and especially the way the police handled moving Oswald from one prison place to another.

Do you think there might be things being held back because of the Kennedy family or because of the children?

I think so. That would be because of the Kennedy children and I don't know, possibly there could be something else that they think that the public would not benefit by knowing it and it possibly could do some harm.

Well, getting back to the assassination and the after effect, did you happen to watch television when they had the body in the Capitol Building and the people were walking by? I think they were lined up for blocks and blocks.

Yes, they were lined up all through the night, I believe, for blocks and blocks and then I remember, I think, it was Ethel Kennedy who came in the evening and went up and visited. And I believe Jackie came and left almost unnoticed or had been in and stopped by the casket and knelt and said a prayer and then left and then it was only after she got outside that they realized that that was who it was that came in. In fact, a good friend of ours was one of the ones that stood in line all night to view the remains.

I guess they had people lined up for miles.

As a matter of fact, I think my brother was there at the time and even went through. Yes, I don't remember now how far back they said the lines went. And I know they were for blocks and from the time they opened it for public viewing [so that] until the time they had to get ready to take it to the church or whenever they stopped the public viewing, the lines were just continuous.

Did you watch the, I guess you'd call it a parade, when they moved the casket down to the Cathedral?

Yes, watched the whole thing. Yes. And when Little John saluted the casket as it was taken out of the church. Yes, I watched all of it that day.

CHRONOLOGY

November 8, 1960 John F. Kennedy is elected the 35th president of the United States.

November 22, 1963 11:40 A.M. (CST) John and Jacqueline Kennedy arrive in Dallas, Texas, aboard Air Force One and leave the airfield in a motorcade.

12:29 P.M. The motorcade enters Dealey Plaza in downtown Dallas.

12:30 P.M. Shots are fired; both Kennedy and Texas Governor John Connally are hit.

12:35 P.M. The presidential car arrives at Parkland Memorial Hospital.

12:36 P.M. The first national news bulletin about the shooting is broadcast by ABC radio. The first television bulletin is broadcast four minutes later by CBS.

1:00 P.M. President Kennedy is pronounced dead after receiving last rites from a Catholic priest.

1:12 P.M. The murder weapon is found at the Texas School Book Depository.

1:15 P.M. Police officer J.D. Tippit is fatally shot by Lee Harvey Oswald.

1:22 P.M. The first unconfirmed announcement of President Kennedy's death is broadcast by CBS radio.

1:38 P.M. The official announcement of Kennedy's death is broadcast by CBS television.

1:55 P.M. Lee Harvard Oswald is arrested for the murder of officer Tippit.

2:18 P.M. President Kennedy's casket is put aboard Air Force One.

2:38 P.M. With Air Force One still on the ground, Lyndon Johnson is sworn in as president by federal judge Sarah Hughes.

5:00 P.M. Air Force One arrives in Washington, D.C.; President Johnson speaks to the nation.

11:26 P.M. Oswald is charged with the murder of Kennedy.

November 23, 1963 President Kennedy's body lies in repose (i.e., for private viewing) in the White House.

Lyndon Johnson, in his first act as president, proclaims Monday, November 25, 1963, a national day of mourning.

November 24, 1963 Lee Harvey Oswald is fatally shot by Jack Ruby during a nationally televised live news broadcast.

President Kennedy's body is taken via horse-drawn caisson to the Capitol Rotunda where it lies in state (i.e., for public viewing) for eighteen hours, during which 250,000 people wait in line and pay their respects.

November 25, 1963 The state funeral for President Kennedy is held. A televised procession of foreign dignitaries and military units marches from the White House to St. Matthew's

Cathedral, where about 1,200 invited guests attend the funeral mass. After another procession, he is buried in Arlington National Cemetery.

November 28, 1963 Thanksgiving Day

November 29, 1963 A commission headed by Supreme Court Chief Justice Earl Warren is appointed by President Lyndon Johnson to investigate the assassination.

September 24, 1964 The Warren Commission releases its report on the assassination of President Kennedy, stating that Lee Harvey Oswald acted alone.

March 14, 1967 The body of President Kennedy is moved about 20 feet to a permanent gravesite more able to accommodate crowds of tourists.

April 23, 1976 The Schweiker-Hart Report, a part of the final report of the United States Senate Select Committee to Study Governmental Operations with Respect to Intelligence Activities (Church Committee), is issued, stating that Kennedy was probably killed by a conspiracy.

September 1976 The United States House of Representatives Select Committee on Assassinations (HSCA) is established to investigate the assassinations of John F. Kennedy and Martin Luther King Jr.

January 2, 1979 The HSCA reports that President Kennedy was probably killed by a conspiracy, but is not able to identify the conspirators.

December 20, 1991 The movie *JFK* is released, reigniting Americans' interest in the assassination and leading to a demand for the release of the complete records of all investigations.

October 26, 1992 The President John F. Kennedy Assassination Records Collection Act of 1992, known as the JFK Records Act, is passed by Congress, directing the National Archives and Records Administration to establish a collection comprising copies of all U.S. government records relating to the assassination. It specifies that all documents except those certified to affect national security must be made public within twenty-five years.

FOR FURTHER READING

Books

Michael Benson, *Who's Who in the JFK Assassination: An A to Z Encyclopedia*. New York: Citadel Press, 1993.

Jim Bishop, *The Day Kennedy Was Shot: An Hour-by-Hour Account of What Really Happened on November 22, 1963*. New York: Funk & Wagnalls, 1968.

Vincent Bugliosi, *Four Days in November: The Assassination of President John F. Kennedy*. New York: Norton, 2008.

Vincent Bugliosi, *Reclaiming History: The Assassination of President John F. Kennedy*. New York: Norton, 2007.

James H. Fetzer, ed., *Murder in Dealey Plaza: What We Know Now That We Didn't Know Then About the Death of JFK*. Chicago: Catfeet Press, 2003.

James H. Fetzer, ed., *The Great Zapruder Film Hoax: Deceit and Deception in the Death of JFK*. Chicago: Catfeet Press, 2003.

Ellen Fitzpatrick, *Letters to Jackie: Condolences from a Grieving Nation*. New York: Ecco, 2010.

Charles Fries and Irv Wilson, eds., *We'll Never Be Young Again: Remembering the Last Days of John F. Kennedy*. Los Angeles: Tallfellow Press, 2003.

Jim Garrison, *On the Trail of the Assassins: My Investigation and Prosecution of the Murder of President Kennedy*. New York: Sheridan Square Press, 1988.

Steven M. Gillon, *The Kennedy Assassination—24 Hours After: Lyndon B. Johnson's Pivotal First Day as President*. New York: Basic Books, 2009.

Henry Hurt, *Reasonable Doubt: An Investigation into the Assassination of John F. Kennedy*. New York: Holt, 1985.

David Kaiser, *The Road to Dallas: The Assassination of John F. Kennedy*. Cambridge, MA: Harvard University Press, 2008.

Peter Knight, *The Kennedy Assassination*. Jackson: University Press of Mississippi, 2007.

Michael L. Kurtz, *Crime of the Century: The Kennedy Assassination from a Historian's Perspective*. Knoxville: University of Tennessee Press, 1993.

Michael L. Kurtz, *The JFK Assassination Debates: Lone Gunman Versus Conspiracy*. Lawrence: University of Kansas Press, 2006.

William Manchester, *The Death of a President: November 20–November 25, 1963*. New York: Harper & Row, 1967.

Jim Marrs, *Crossfire: The Plot That Killed Kennedy*. New York: Carroll & Graf, 1989.

Gerald D. McKnight, *Breach of Trust: How the Warren Commission Failed the Nation and Why*. Lawrence: University Press of Kansas, 2005.

Ion Mihai Pacepa, *Programmed to Kill: Lee Harvey Oswald, the Soviet KGB, and the Kennedy Assassination*. Chicago: Ivan R. Dee, 2007.

James Piereson, *Camelot and the Cultural Revolution: How the Assassination of John F. Kennedy Shattered American Liberalism*. New York: Encounter Books, 2007.

Gerald Posner, *Case Closed: Lee Harvey Oswald and the Assassination of JFK*. New York: Random House, 1993.

Gus Russo and Stephen Molton, *Brothers in Arms: The Kennedys, the Castros, and the Politics of Murder*. New York: Bloomsbury, 2009.

Robert B. Semple, ed., *Four Days in November: The Original Coverage of the John F. Kennedy Assassination*. New York: St. Martin's, 2003.

Larry A. Sneed, *No More Silence: An Oral History of the Assassination of President Kennedy*. Denton: University of North Texas Press, 2002.

Lamar Waldron, *Legacy of Secrecy: The Long Shadow of the JFK Assassination*. Berkeley, CA: Counterpoint, 2009.

The Warren Commission Report: Report of the President's Commission on the Assassination of President John F. Kennedy (unabridged edition). New York: St. Martin's, 1992.

David R. Wrone, *The Zapruder Film: Reframing JFK's Assassination*. Lawrence: University Press of Kansas, 2003.

Barbie Zeller, *Covering the Body: The Kennedy Assassination, the Media, and the Shaping of Collective Memory*. Chicago: University of Chicago Press, 1992.

Periodicals

David W. Belin, "The Warren Commission: Why We Still Don't Believe It," *New York Times Magazine*, November 20, 1988.

Ralph Blumenthal, "40 Years After Shots in Dallas, a Survivor's Painful Memories," *New York Times*, October 31, 2003.

"Did the Mob Kill J.F.K.?" *Time*, June 21, 2007.

Roger Ebert, review of *JFK*, *Chicago Sun-Times*, December 20, 1991.

Paul Findley, "In Kennedy Assassination, Anyone but Mossad Is Fair Game for U.S. Media," *Washington Report on Middle East Affairs*, March 1992. Available at www.wrmea.com/backissues/0392/9203026.html.

Ben A. Franklin, "250,000 Mourners File Silently Past Coffin in Capitol's Rotunda During 18 Hours," *New York Times*, November 26, 1963.

Max Holland, "The Lie That Linked CIA to the Kennedy Assassination," *Studies in Intelligence*, Fall/Winter 2001. Available at www.cia.gov/library/center-for-the-study-of-intelligence/csi-publications/csi-studies/studies/fall_winter_2001/article02.html.

"J.F.K.: The Murder & the Myths," *Time*, June 12, 1964.

"JFK Assassination: Your Memories," CNN.com, November 22, 2003. www.cnn.com/2003/US/11/19/ys.jfk.1.

George Lardner, Jr., "How Oliver Stone's Version of the Kennedy Assassination Exploits the Edge of Paranoia," *Washington Post*, May 19, 1991.

William E. Leuchtenburg, "John F. Kennedy, Twenty Years Later," *American Heritage*, December 1983.

Thomas Mallon, "A Knoll of One's Own," *Atlantic*, June 2007.

Karl E. Meyer, "1963: History as Tragedy," *New Statesman*, December 6, 1999.

William Plummer, David Grogan, and Denise Lynch, "Where We Were," *People*, November 28, 1968.

Richard H. Popkin, "Garrison's Case," *New York Review of Books*, September 14, 1967.

Ron Rosenbaum, "Taking a Darker View," *Time*, January 13, 1992.

"Shadow on a Grassy Knoll," *Time*, May 26, 1967.

Christopher Shennon, "The Day the Lights Went Out: Kennedy Assassination," *London Times*, October 22, 1988.

Philip Shenon, "Who Killed John Kennedy? After 25 Years, More Theories Than Certainty," *New York Times*, November 18, 1988.

Mark Steyn, "What Rot—It Was So Not Camelot," *MacLean's*, August 13, 2007.

Cal Thomas, "JFK, Plus 40," *Jewish World Review*, November 18, 2003.

George Weigel, "The Sixties, Again and Again," *First Things*, April 2008.

Theodore H. White, "For President Kennedy, an Epilogue," *Life*, December 6, 1963.

"Willful Misunderstanding: When JFK Was Assassinated, Liberals Couldn't Stand the Truth. Can They Now?" *Weekly Standard*, November 23, 2009.

Timothy P. Yu, "Sharing in the Kennedy Mystique," *Harvard Crimson*, November 22, 1993.

Web Sites

Assassination Archives and Research Center (www.aarc library.org/aarc.htm). An organization whose holdings comprise the most extensive collection of records on the Kennedy assassination in private hands. It has approximately 1,500 books on assassinations and related topics including newspaper and magazine articles, unpublished manuscripts, trial transcripts, and other material, some of which is online.

History Matters (www.history-matters.com/archive/contents/contents-jfk.htm). An archive of voluminous electronic holdings related to the murder of President Kennedy and the subsequent investigations of that crime. It offers tens of thousands of pages of reports, transcripts, and other documents, as well as dozens of hours of audio segments.

JFK Assassination Resources Online (www.jfk-online.com). A site maintained by a researcher who is considered one of the best working on assassination issues. It contains a large amount of material, including commentary related to the Garrison investigation.

JFK Lancer (www.jfklancer.com). A historical research company specializing in the presidency and assassination of President John F. Kennedy. Its site includes documents and many video and audio clips.

John F. Kennedy Assassination Homepage (www.jfk-assassination.de). A German site (in English) containing many resources, including, among other things, the testimony given to the Warren Commission and audio files of radio reports broadcast live at the time of the assassination.

John F. Kennedy Presidential Library and Museum (www.jfklibrary.org). The official Kennedy presidential library administered by the National Archives and Records Administration. Its site contains essays about historical events during his administration plus a section for students with many articles about Kennedy and biographies of people associated with his presidency.

John F. Kennedy Presidential Library YouTube Channel (www.youtube.com/user/JFKLF). A YouTube channel maintained by the official Kennedy library, containing videos of

Kennedy, including his inaugural speech and excerpts from many others.

Kennedy Assassination Home Page (http://mcadams.posc.mu.edu). A large searchable site dedicated to debunking misinformation and disinformation surrounding the murder of JFK. It contains articles countering prevalent myths about Kennedy and about the assassination, book reviews, and a long annotated list of links to other assassination sites worth visiting.

Mary Ferrell Foundation (www.maryferrell.org). A nonprofit organization maintaining the world's largest searchable electronic collection of materials related to the JFK assassination—more than 1,300,000 pages of scanned reports and documents, as well as essays initially published at the site.

President John F. Kennedy Assassination Records (www.archives.gov/research/jfk). A site maintained by the National Archives. The full texts of the Warren Commission Report and the report of the House Select Committee on Assassinations (HSCA) are available here, along with other searchable material.

Sixth Floor Museum at Dealey Plaza (www.jfk.org). A historical museum located on the sixth and seventh floors of the warehouse known in 1963 as the Texas School Book Depository. Its site contains videos, including the Zapruder Film, as well as pictures and information about visits to the museum.

INDEX

L

M

P

R

S

T

Y

Z